Inauguration of Auroville

28 February 1968 - 28 February 2018

Copyright : Prisma, Auroville
Author : Franz Fassbender
Photographs : John Mandeen

First edition: 2013

ISBN: 978-93-95460-27-9 (Print)
ISBN: 978-93-95460-22-4 (ebook)

BISAC Code:
HIS062000, HISTORY / Asia / South / India
HIS037070, HISTORY / Modern / 20th Century /General
HIS030000, HISTORY / Reference

Thema Subject Category:
JBS, Social groups, communities and identities
NH, History
NHF, Asian history
NHT, History: specific events and topics
NHTB, Social and cultural history

Cataloging-in-Publication Data for this title is available from the Library of Congress.

Digital Editions produced by:
DMI Systems Pvt Ltd, Vishnupuri,
Aligarh 202001, Uttar Pradesh, India
www.dmi.systems

Published by:
PRISMA, Aurelec/ Prayogshala, Auroville
605101, Tamil Nadu, India
www.prisma.haus

Acknowledgements

The texts by Sri Aurobindo and the Mother are copyright of the Sri Aurobindo Ashram Trust, Pondicherry, and are reproduced here with acknowledgement and thanks to the Trustees. The copyright holder for Mother's Agenda is "Institut de Recherches Evolutives", Paris.

Contents

The concept of human unity in diversity, and Auroville

There are records from 1912 onwards, specifically in Sri Aurobindo's writings, indicating that for human unity to eventually manifest on Planet Earth there would be an initial need – at a certain stage of humanity's evolution – for an experimental international-universal township to be established, where people from around the world could live together following a higher and truer life than had been achieved up to then; a life not following any existing or future religion but with a spiritual basis.

'A Dream' and an opportunity for its realisation

Over the years the Mother wrote about or spoke on many important topics, but of special significance is the short text she produced in 1954 titled 'A Dream', as follows:

There should be somewhere upon earth a place that no nation could claim as its sole property, a place where all human beings of good will, sincere in their aspiration, could live freely as citizens of the world, obeying one single authority, that of the supreme Truth; a place of peace, concord, harmony, where all the fighting instincts of man would be used exclusively to conquer the causes of his suffering and misery, to surmount his weakness and ignorance, to triumph over his limitations and incapacities; a place where the needs of the spirit and the care for progress would get precedence over the satisfaction of desires and passions, the seeking for pleasures and material enjoyment.

In this place, children would be able to grow and develop integrally without losing contact with their soul. Education would be given, not with a view to passing examinations and getting certificates and posts, but for enriching the existing faculties and bringing forth new ones. In this place, titles and positions would be supplanted by opportunities to serve and organise.

The needs of the body will be provided for equally in the case of each and every one. In the general organisation intellectual, moral and spiritual superiority will find expression not in the enhancement of the pleasures and powers of life but in the increase of duties and responsibilities. Artistic beauty in all forms, painting, sculpture, music, literature, will be available equally to all, the opportunity to share in the joys they bring being limited solely by each one's capacities and not by one's social or financial position.

For in this ideal place money would be no more the sovereign lord. Individual merit will have a greater importance than the value due to material wealth and social position. Work would not be there as the means of gaining one's livelihood, it would be the means whereby to express oneself, develop one's capacities and possibilities, while doing at the same time service to the whole group, which on its side would provide for each one's subsistence and for the field of his work.

In brief, it would be a place where relations between human beings, usually based almost exclusively upon competition and strife, would be replaced by relations of emulation for doing better, for collaboration, relations of real brotherhood.

In this text she describes the sort of ideal society that Sri Aurobindo had envisaged as a first step towards human unity. She added, however, a footnote to the effect that humanity didn't yet possess at that time the power and knowledge to realize the ideal portrayed, which threw up inevitable questions such as when, where, and on what basis could such an extremely ambitious, globally important and potentially world-transforming project be launched?

Ten years later, on 14th August 1964, during the 1st World Conference of the Sri Aurobindo Society (SAS) in Pondicherry, the then General Secretary Sri Navajata presented the idea of developing "a township near Pondicherry, with all the amenities and facilities for residence and work for those who want to prepare for a better life." The outcome was a resolution passed in favour of starting the project, which was subsequently put before The Mother – as President of the SAS – for her approval. She gave her Blessings, and thus the concept of Auroville first came into being.

Auroville located in Tamil Nadu

Auroville, which is located in Tamil Nadu, close to the Coromandel Coast, was started in 1968. As a physical entity it is planned to be only around 5 kms in diameter inclusive of a surrounding Green Belt. Back in 1968, the land was already denuded of nearly all vegetation, and frequent dust storms and monsoon deluges stripped it further of its meagre topsoil, carving ravines as rainwater poured down from the plateau into the sea. The local villagers were living in small palm-leaf thatched huts, and in some families the women could come out only one at a time because there was only one saree to wear between them. In some villages they had to walk 2 kms to fetch water. Most were eating only a gruel made of the millets which they were growing on their infertile fields, and they were looking malnourished. But they had hope. Many responded to the call of the Mother to sell their lands to Auroville, and they were eager to work, which they were able to do even in the hot sun. They were also ready to learn new skills, a new language, new ways of living.

The Divine Life

At present mankind is undergoing an evolutionary crisis in which is concealed a choice of its destiny; for a stage has been reached in which the human mind has achieved in certain directions an enormous development while in others it stands arrested and bewildered and can no longer find its way.

A structure of the external life has been raised up by man's ever active mind and life-will, a structure of an unmanageable hugeness and complexity, for the service of his mental, vital, physical claims and urges, a complex political, social, administrative, economic, cultural machinery, an organised collective means for his intellectual, sensational, aesthetic and material satisfaction.

Man has created a system of civilization which has become too big for his limited mental capacity and understanding and his still more limited spiritual and moral capacity to utilise and manage, a too dangerous servant of his blundering ego and its appetites. For no greater seeing mind, no intuitive soul of knowledge has yet come to his surface of consciousness which could make this basic fullness of life a condition for the free growth of something that exceeded it.

This new fullness of the means of life might be, by its power for a release from the incessant unsatisfied stress of his economic and physical needs, an opportunity for the full pursuit of other and greater aims surpassing the material existence, for the discovery of a higher truth and good and beauty, for the discovery of a greater and diviner spirit which would intervene and use life for a higher

perfection of the being: but it is being used instead for the multiplication of new wants and an aggressive expansion of the collective ego.

At the same time Science has put at his disposal many potencies of the universal Force and has made the life of humanity materially one; but what uses this universal Force is a little human individual or communal ego with nothing universal in its light of knowledge or its movements, no inner sense or power which would create in this physical drawing together of the human world a true life-unity, a mental unity or a spiritual oneness.

All that is there is a chaos of clashing mental ideas, urges of individual and collective physical want and need, vital claims and desires, impulses of an ignorant life-push, hungers and calls for life satisfaction of individuals, classes, nations, a rich fungus of political and social and economic nostrums and notions, a hustling medley of slogans and panaceas for which men are ready to oppress and be oppressed, to kill and be killed, to impose them somehow or other by the immense and too formidable means placed at his disposal, in the belief that this is his way out to something ideal.

The evolution of human mind and life must necessarily lead towards an increasing universality; but on a basis of ego and segmenting and dividing mind this opening to the universal can only create a vast pullulation of unaccorded ideas and impulses, a surge of enormous powers and desires, a chaotic mass of unassimilated and intermixed mental, vital and physical material of a larger existence which, because it is not taken up by a creative harmonising

light of the Spirit, must welter in a universalised confusion and discord out of which it is impossible to build a greater harmonic life.

Man has harmonised life in the past by organised ideation and limitation; he has created societies based on fixed ideas or fixed customs, a fixed cultural system or an organic life-system, each with its own order; the throwing of all these into the melting-pot of a more and more intermingling life and a pouring in of ever new ideas and motives and facts and possibilities call for a new, a greater consciousness to meet and master the increasing potentialities of existence and harmonise them.

Reason and Science can only help by standardising, by fixing everything into an artificially arranged and mechanised unity of material life. A greater whole-being, whole-knowledge, whole-power is needed to weld all into a greater unity of whole-life.

A life of unity, mutuality and harmony born of a deeper and wider truth of our being is the only truth of life that can successfully replace the imperfect mental constructions of the past, which were a combination of association and regulated conflict, an accommodation of egos and interests grouped or dovetailed into each other to form a society, a consolidation by common general life-motives, a unification by need and the pressure of struggle with outside forces. It is such a change and such a reshaping of life for which humanity is blindly beginning to seek, now more and more with a sense that its very existence depends upon finding the way.

Sri Aurobindo, The Life Divine

Courage
and love
are the only
indispensable
virtues;
even if
all the others
are eclipsed
or fall asleep,
these two
will save
the soul
alive.

Sri Aurobindo
Thoughts and Aphorisms

Courage
Bold, it faces all dangers.

Historical aspects of Auroville

Although Auroville is a township under construction, the landscape in which it is situated has already had countless previous incarnations and avatars. Of special interest to Aurovilians is the fact that a few kilometres away is its 'mother-town', Pondicherry, the home of Sri Aurobindo and the Mother, the site of the Sri Aurobindo Ashram.

The origins of Pondicherry go back to the mists of time. The original name of the town, no longer used, was Vedapuri, and a big temple still stands today, the Vedapurishwara temple, dedicated to the great god Siva, the god of the contemplatives. Vedapuri means 'city of knowledge'. The patron saint of Vedapuri was Sri Agastya, who according to legend came from the far Himalayas, travelling south, to settle in the country of the Tamils and teach the people the Veda. For thousands of years, Vedapuri was a school for young Brahmins where they learned to chant the Vedic hymns in Sanskrit and to perform complicated rituals in the proper way.

Buddhism came and went, and then in the first and second centuries of our era we find on that same Coromandel Coast a Roman settlement mentioned in the *Periple* by Ptolemy of Alexandria. Heavily loaded ships came from the far Mediterranean, swept by the constant trade winds, to arrive via Cleopatra's Nile-Red Sea Canal at Poduke, as the town was then called. It was a Roman emporium, a trader's town where Mediterranean wines and swords, Germanic slaves and Roman gold were exchanged for the spices and

Herdsmen and children guiding cows and goats through the canyon landscape of early Auroville.
Palmyra trees were the first and virtually only trees in the barren landscape.

silks, precious stones, cottons and peacocks of India. The poet-prince Ilango, brother of the Chera king Kovalan, describes how – like some future Auroville – it appeared in the first century, in the following text, which is translated from the original picturesque Tamil.

"The sun shone over the open terraces, over the warehouses near the harbour, and over the turrets with their air-holes like the eyes of the deer (a description of windows built with a Roman arch). In different places the observer's attention was arrested by the sight of Yavanas (a name for Greeks and Romans) whose prosperity never waned.

"In the harbour were to be seen sailing vessels with many sailors from distant lands. To all appearances they lived as one community. In the streets of the city hawkers went about with cosmetics, bath powders, cool pastes, flowers, incense and fragrant perfumes. In certain places weavers were seen dealing in fine fabrics of silk, animal hair and cotton. Whole streets were full of cloth, corals, sandalwood and myrrh, besides a wealth of rare ornaments, perfect pearls, gems and gold beyond all reckoning."

The description of the city itself and the central highway leading to it also has its poetic charm: "Entering into the central highway of the city, rich with the wealth of sea-borne goods and reaching down to the seashore where flags of foreign countries fly high, one is impressed by these stretches of white sand where are displayed various kinds of goods brought in by ships of foreign merchants who have left their homes and settled here.

"Here, burning in the evening, were myriads of lamps: lamps of those who sold coloured powders, who sold

The Auroville landscape – early days.

sandalwood, jasmine flowers, scents, and all varieties of sweets; the lamps of dexterous goldsmiths, and of those who, sitting in a row, sold pittu; the broad black lamps placed on lampstands by the sellers of muffins; the lamps of fishmongers glimmering here and there; and high above all, the bright beacon lights erected to guide ships to the shore.

"There were lamps taken out to sea by fishermen in their boats as they went with their nets, night-long lights set out by foreigners speaking strange languages, and finally the lamps lit by the watchmen of the warehouses containing valuable merchandise from far away countries."

Recent archaeological excavations of a low hill called Arikamedu south of Pondicherry have yielded Greek and Roman coins and imported Mediterranean pottery, reminiscent of a trade very much to the detriment of the Roman empire.

Such was the eagerness of Roman ladies to possess the colourful silks and fine muslins of India that Rome lost much of its gold reserves in this exchange, but it benefited the kings of the Coromandel Coast, who became fabulously rich and were able to build the huge temple towns of Rameswaram and Chidambaram, of Madurai and Trichinopoly, and – less than a hundred miles from where Auroville is being built – the magnificent Versailles of India, Mahabalipuram.

Vedapuri itself fell asleep. The destructive force of Islam came and went; the Portuguese came and called the town 'Puducheira', and the Dutch 'Poeleser', and the Danes – all trying to get some of the gold the Romans had lost – and built their trading posts, their 'comptoirs'.

Children make their way across a stark open landscape.

In the 17th century came the French, who built on the shore the largest and most powerful fortress in southern India. As a fortress it was very successful; also as a safe place for investments in gold during troubled times. It quickly became rich, too rich for the jealous British in Madras, who razed it to the ground.

Rebuilt in the 18th century in the French provincial style, the town could be seen from the plateau of Auroville, now a part of free India.

Only a few small fishermen's villages without history stand today where the 20th century, with its big bulldozers, is moving in to build the city of a new dawn.

Equals One

A lone woman heads home along an eroded earth road.

An early conversation with Mother on Auroville

Have you heard of Auroville?

For a long time, I had a plan of the "ideal town", but that was during Sri Aurobindo's lifetime, with Sri Aurobindo living at the centre. Afterwards, I was no longer interested. Then the idea of Auroville — I gave the name Auroville — was taken up again, but from the other end: instead of the formation having to find the place, it was the place — near the lake — which gave birth to the formation, and until now I took only a very minor interest in it, for I had received nothing directly. Then our little A. took it into her head to have a house there, by the lake, and to have a house for me next to hers, and to offer it to me. And she wrote me all her dreams: one or two sentences suddenly stirred an old, old memory of something which had tried to manifest — a creation — when I was very young and which had again started trying to manifest at the very beginning of the century, when I was with Théon. Then all that was forgotten. It came back with this letter; all at once, I had my plan for Auroville. Now I have my overall plan, I am waiting for B. to draw the detailed plans, for I had said from the beginning: "B. will be the architect", and I wrote to B. When he came here last year, he went to see Chandigarh, the town built by Le Corbusier, up there in the Punjab, and he was not very happy. It seems quite ordinary to me — I know nothing about it, I haven't seen it, I only saw some photographs which were horrible. And while he was speaking to me, I could see that he felt, "Oh, if only I had a town to build! . . ." So I wrote to him: "If you want, I have a town to build." He is happy. He is

One of the earlier concepts of the future town plan.

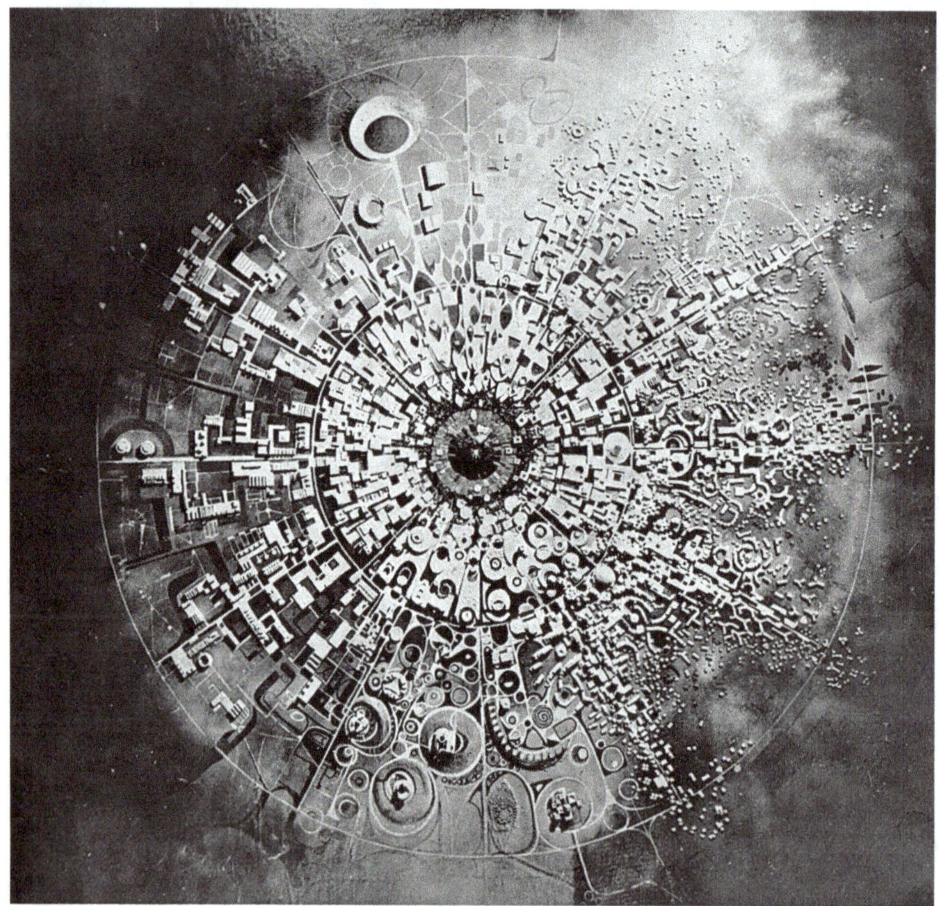

coming. When he comes, I shall show him my plan and he will build the town. My plan is very simple.

The place is up there, on the Madras road, on top of the hill. (Mother takes a paper and begins to draw.) We have here — naturally, it is not like that in Nature, we shall have to adapt ourselves; it is like that up there on the ideal plane — here, a central point. This central point is a park which I saw when I was very young — perhaps the most beautiful thing in the world from the point of view of physical, material Nature — a park with water and trees, like all parks, and flowers, but not many; flowers in the form of creepers, palms and ferns, all varieties of palms; water, if possible running water, and possibly a small cascade. From the practical point of view, it would be very good: at the far end, outside the park, we could build reservoirs which would be used to supply water to the residents.

So in this park, I saw the "Pavilion of Love". But I dislike this word, for man has turned it into something grotesque; I am speaking of the principle of Divine Love. But that has changed: it will be "The Pavilion of Mother" – but not this (Mother points to herself) — the Mother, the true Mother, the principle of the Mother. I say "Mother" because Sri Aurobindo used that word, otherwise I would have put something else, I would have put "creative principle" or "principle of realisation" or — I do not know. . . . It will be a small building, not a big one, with only a meditation room downstairs, but with columns and probably a circular shape. I say probably, because I am leaving that for B. to decide. Upstairs, the first floor will be a room and the roof will be a covered terrace. You know the ancient Indo-Moghul miniatures, with palaces where there are terraces with small roofs

The Mother with Prime Minister Pandit Jawaharlal Nehru, Kumarasami Kamaraj, Indira Gandhi and Lal Bahadur Shastri (1955).

supported by columns? You know those old miniatures? Hundreds of them have come into my hands. . . . But this pavilion is very, very beautiful, a small pavilion like this, with a roof on a terrace, and low walls with couches against them to sit on, to meditate in the open air in the evening, at night. And below, downstairs, at ground-level, a meditation room, simply — something quite bare. There would probably be at the far end something which would be a living light, perhaps the symbol in living light, a constant light. Otherwise, a very peaceful, very silent place.

Nearby, there would be a small dwelling, a small dwelling which would nevertheless have three floors, but not large-sized, and that would be the house of A, who would serve as a guardian. She would be the guardian of the pavilion. She wrote me a very nice letter but she did not understand all that, of course.

That is the centre.

All around, there is a circular road which separates the park from the rest of the town. There would probably be a gateway — in fact there must be one — in the park. A gateway with the guardian of the gate. The guardian of the gate is a new girl who has come from Africa, who wrote me a letter telling me that she wanted to be the guardian of Auroville in order to let only the "servants of Truth" enter (Mother laughs). It is a very nice plan. So I shall probably put her there as guardian of the park, with a small house on the road at the entrance.

But the interesting thing is that around this central point, there are four big sections, like four big petals (Mother draws), but the corners of the petals are rounded and there are small intermediate zones — four big

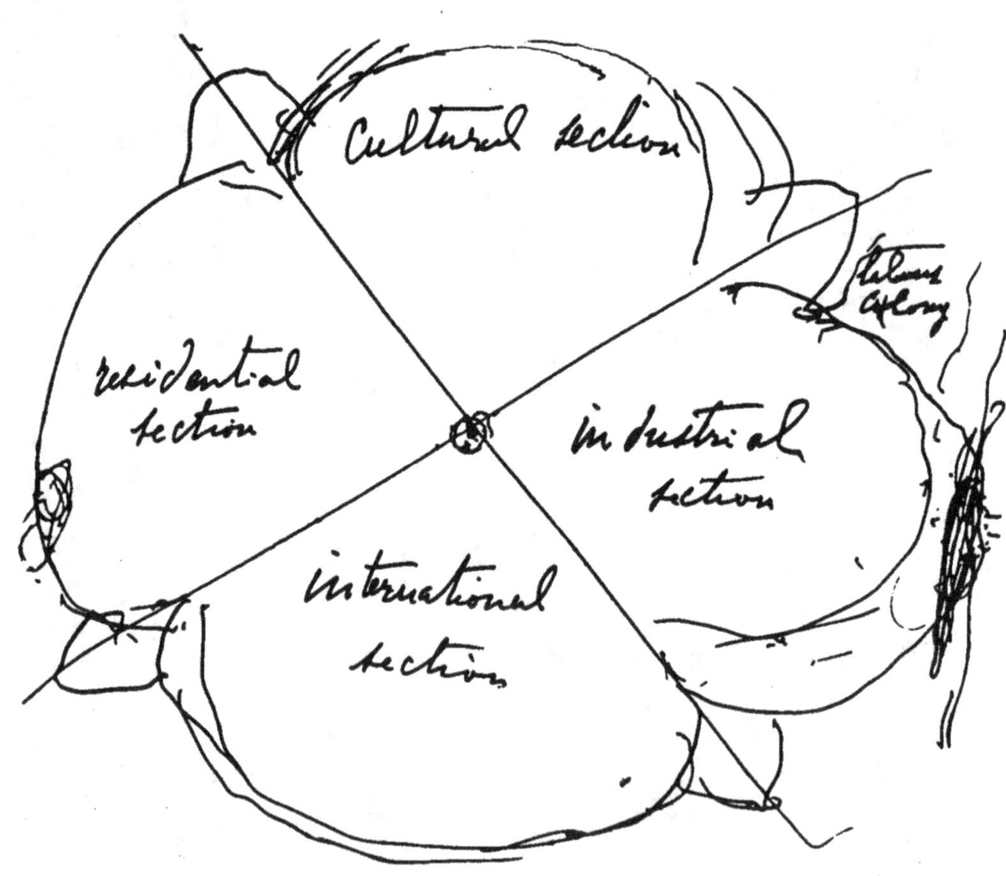

sections and four zones. Naturally that is only in the air; on the ground, it will be an approximation.

We have four big sections: the cultural section, to the North, that is to say, towards Madras; to the East, the industrial section; to the South, the international section; and to the West, that is to say, towards the lake, the residential section.

To make myself clear: the residential section, where there will be the houses of the people who have already subscribed and of all the others who are coming in large numbers to have a plot in Auroville. That will be next to the lake.

The international section: we have already approached a certain number of ambassadors and countries for each one to have its pavilion — a pavilion from every country. It was an old idea. Some have already accepted, so it is on the way. Each pavilion has its own garden with, as far as possible, representation of the plants and products of the country which it represents. If they have enough money and enough space, they can also have a sort of small museum or permanent exhibition of the country's achievements. The buildings should be constructed according to the architecture of each country — it should be like a document of information. Then, depending on the money they wish to spend, they could also have accommodation for students, conference rooms, etc., a cuisine of the country, a restaurant of the country — they could have all kinds of developments.

Then the industrial section. Already many people, including the Government of Madras — the Madras Government is loaning money — want to start industries, which will be on a special basis.

This industrial section is to the East and it is very big, there is plenty of space; it will go down towards the sea. In fact, to the North of Pondicherry there is quite a large area which is totally uninhabited and uncultivated; it is by the sea, going up the coast towards the North. So this industrial section would go down towards the sea, and if possible there would be a kind of wharf — not exactly a port but a place where boats could come alongside; and all these industries, with the inland transportation they need, would have a possibility to export directly. And there, there would be a big hotel — B. has already made a plan for it; we wanted to build the hotel here, on the site of the "Messageries Maritimes", but after having said yes, the owner said no; it is very good, it will be better over there — a big hotel to receive visitors from outside. Already quite a number of industries have registered for this section; I do not know if there will be enough room, but we shall manage.

Then, to the North — that is where there is the most space, of course — towards Madras, the cultural section. There, an auditorium — the auditorium which I have dreamt of building for a long time; plans had already been made — an auditorium with a concert-hall and a grand organ, the best of its kind today. It seems they are making wonderful things. I want a grand organ. There will also be a stage with wings — a rotating stage, etc., the best of its kind. So, a magnificent auditorium, there. There will be a library, there will be a museum with all sorts of exhibitions — not inside the auditorium: in addition to it there will be a film-studio, a film-school; there will be a gliding club. Already we almost have authorisation from the Government, and the promise, so it is already well on the way. Then towards Madras, where there is plenty of space, a stadium. We want this stadium to be the most modern and the most perfect possible, with the idea — it is an idea I have had for a long time — that twelve years — the Olympic Games take place every four years — twelve years from 1968 — in '68 the Olympiads are taking place in Mexico — twelve years later we would hold the Olympic Games in India, there. So we need space.

Between these sections, there are intermediate zones, four intermediate zones: one for public services, post office, etc.; one zone for transport, railway station and possibly an aerodrome; one zone for food — that one would be near the lake and would include dairies, poultry farms, orchards, cultivated lands, etc.; it would spread and include the Lake Estate: what they wanted to do separately would be within the framework of Auroville. Then a fourth zone. I have said: public services, transport, food, and the fourth zone: shops. We do not need many shops, but a few are necessary in order to obtain what we do not produce. They are like districts, you see.

And you will be there at the centre?

A. hopes so (Mother laughs). I did not say no, I did not say yes; I told her, "The Lord will decide." It depends on my state of health. A removal, no — I am here because of the Samadhi, I shall stay here, that is quite sure. But I can go there on a visit; it is not so far, it takes five minutes by car. But A. wants to be quiet, silent, aloof, and that is quite possible in her park, surrounded by a road, with someone to stop people from coming in; one can stay very quiet — but if I am there, that is the end of it! There would be collective meditations, etc. That is to say that if I get a sign, first the physical sign, then the inner command to go out, I shall drive there and spend an hour, in the afternoon — I can do that now and then. We still have time because, before everything is ready, it will take years.

That is to say that the disciples will stay here?

Ah! The Ashram stays here — the Ashram stays here, I stay here, that is understood. Auroville is...

A satellite

Yes, it is the contact with the outside world. The centre on my drawing is a symbolic centre.

But that is what A. expects: she wants a house where she would be all alone next to a house where I would be all alone. The second part is a dream, because myself all alone. . . . You only have to see what is happening! It is true, isn't it? So it does not go with the "all alone". Solitude must be found within, it is the only way. But as far as living is concerned, I shall certainly not go and live there, because the Samadhi is here; but I could go there to visit. For example, I could go there for an inauguration or for certain ceremonies. We shall see. It will be years from now.

In short, Auroville is more for outside?

Oh yes! It is a town! Consequently, it is the whole contact with outside. An attempt to realise on earth a more ideal life.

In the old formation which I had made, there had to be a hill and a river. There had to be a hill, because Sri Aurobindo's house was on top of the hill. But Sri Aurobindo was there at the centre. It was arranged according to the plan of my symbol, that is to say, a point in the middle, with Sri Aurobindo and all that concerned Sri Aurobindo's life, and four big petals — which were not the same as on this drawing, it was something else — and twelve all around, the town itself; and around that, there were the residences of the disciples; you know my symbol: instead of lines, there are bands; well, the last circular band formed the area for the disciples' residences, and each one had his own house and garden — a small house and a garden for each one. There was some means of transport, I wasn't sure if it was individual transport or collective transport — like those small open tramcars in the mountains, you know — going in all directions to take the disciples back towards the centre of the town. And around all that, there was a wall, with a gateway and guardians at the gate, and one could not enter without authorisation. There was no money — within the walls, no money; at the various entrances, there were banks or counters of some sort, where people could deposit their money and receive tickets in exchange, with which they could obtain lodging, food, this, that. But no money — the tickets were only for visitors, who could not enter without a permit. It was a tremendous organisation. . . . No money, I did not want any money.

Look! In my plan I forgot one thing. I wanted to build a housing estate for workers, but the housing estate was to be part of the industrial section, perhaps an extension along the edge of the industrial section.

Outside the walls, in my first formation, on one side there was an industrial town, and on the other, fields, farms, etc., to supply the town. But that represented a real country — not a big country, but a country.

Now it is much reduced. It is no longer my symbol; there are only four zones and there are no walls. And there will be money. You see, the other formation was truly an ideal endeavour. . . . But I counted on many years before trying to start. At that time I thought twenty-four years. But now it is much more modest, it is a transitional attempt, and it is much more realisable. The other plan was. . . I almost had the land; it was in the time of Sir Akbar, you remember, from Hyderabad. They sent me some photographs of the State of Hyderabad and there, in those photographs, I found my ideal spot: an isolated hill, quite a big hill, and below it, a large, flowing river. I told him, "I want this place", and he arranged the matter. Everything was arranged. They sent me the plans, the papers and everything, saying that they were giving it to the Ashram. But they laid down one condition — it was virgin forest, uncultivated land — the place was given on condition, naturally, that we would cultivate it — but the products must be utilised on the spot; for example, the crops, the wood, must be utilised on the spot, not transported; nothing could leave the State of Hyderabad. There was even C, who was a navigator, who said that he would obtain a sailing boat from England to go up the river to fetch the products and bring them to us here. Everything was very well planned! Then they set this condition. I asked if it was not possible to have it removed; then Sir Akbar died and that was the end of it, the matter was dropped. Afterwards, I was glad that it was not done because, now that Sri Aurobindo has departed, I cannot leave Pondicherry. I could only leave Pondicherry with him provided that he accepted to live in his ideal town. At that time, I had spoken of this project to D, the person who built Golconde; and he was enthusiastic, he told me, "As soon as you start to build, call me, I shall come." I had shown him my plan; it was based on an enlargement of my symbol; he was most enthusiastic, he thought it was magnificent.

It was dropped. But the other one, which is just a small intermediate attempt, we can try.

I have no illusions that it will keep its original purity, but we shall try something.

The Mother

The flowers of Auroville

Mother chose a variety of hibiscus which she had already called "Beauty of Supramental Love" as the symbol of Auroville and she made the following comment: "It urges us to live at its height".

The first hibiscus chosen by Mother as the emblem of Auroville was "Godhead", of which she wrote: "Pure and perfect, projects its force into the world". It is a large single flower of the Hawaiian variety, cream in colour with a rose centre and crinkled petals.

But later on, seeing another variety, "Beauty of Supramental Love", she gave it first place, because this flower is almost the same colour as the earth of Auroville. "Godhead" remains nevertheless one of the flowers of Auroville.

Mother also chose special hibiscus flowers for most of the gardens which will surround the Matrimandir. Later on she attributed special qualities of Auroville to several varieties of hibiscus.

I invite you to the great adventure

Well, I announced to you all that this new world was born. But it has been so engulfed, as it were, in the old world that so far the difference has not been very perceptible to many people. Still, the action of the new forces has continued very regularly, very persistently, very steadily, and to a certain extent, very effectively.

And one of the manifestations of this action was my experience – truly so very new – of yesterday evening. And the result of all this I have noted step by step in almost daily experiences. It could be expressed succinctly, in a rather linear way.

First, it is not only a "new conception" of spiritual life and the divine Reality. This conception, which was expressed by Sri Aurobindo, I have expressed myself many a time, and it could be formulated somewhat like this: the old spirituality was an escape from life into the divine Reality, leaving the world just where it was, as it was; whereas our new vision, on the contrary, is a divinisation of life, a transformation of the material world into a divine world. This has been said, repeated, more or less understood, indeed it is the basic idea of what we want to do. But this could be a continuation with an improvement, a widening of the old world as it was – and so long as this is a conception up there in the field of thought, in fact it is hardly more than that – but what has happened, the really new thing, is that a new world is born, born, born. It is not the old one transforming itself, it is a new world which is born. And we are right in the midst of this period of transition where the two are entangled – where the other still persists all-powerful and entirely dominating the ordinary consciousness, but where the new one is quietly slipping in, still very modest, unnoticed – unnoticed to the extent that outwardly it doesn't disturb anything very much, for the time being, and that in the consciousness of most people it is even altogether imperceptible. And yet it is working, growing – until it is strong enough to assert itself visibly.

In any case, to simplify things, it could be said that characteristically the old world, the creation of what Sri Aurobindo calls the Overmind, was an age of the gods, and consequently the age of religions. As I said, the flower of human effort towards what is above it gave rise to innumerable religious forms, to a religious relationship between the best souls and the invisible world. And at the very summit of all that, as an effort towards a higher realization, there has arisen the idea of the unity of religions, of this "one single thing" which is behind all these manifestations; and this idea has truly been, so to speak, the extreme limit of human aspiration. Well, that is at the frontier, it is something that still belongs completely to the Overmind world, the Overmind creation, and which from there seems to be looking towards this "other thing" which is a new creation it cannot grasp – which it tries to reach, feels coming, but cannot grasp. To grasp it, a reversal is needed. It is necessary to leave the Overmind creation. It was necessary that the new creation, the Supramental creation should take place.

And now, all these old things seem so old, so out-of-date, so arbitrary – such a travesty of the real truth. In the Supramental creation there will no longer be any religions. The whole life will be the expression, the flowering into forms of the divine Unity manifesting in the world. And there will no longer be what men now call gods.

These great divine beings themselves will be able to participate in the new creation; but to do so, they will have to put on what we could call the "Supramental substance" on earth. And if some of them choose to remain in their world as they are, if they decide not to manifest physically, their relation with the beings of a Supramental earth will be a relation of friends, collaborators, equals, for the highest divine essence will be manifested in the beings of the new Supramental world on earth.

When the physical substance is Supramentalised, to incarnate on earth will no longer be a cause of inferiority, quite the contrary. It will give a plenitude which cannot be obtained otherwise.

But all this is in the future; it is a future... which has begun, but which will take some time to be realised integrally. Meanwhile we are in a very special situation, extremely special, without precedent. We are now witnessing the birth of a new world; it is very young, very weak – not in its essence but in its outer manifestation – not yet recognised, not even felt, denied by the majority. But it is here. It is here, making an effort to grow, absolutely sure of the result. But the road to it is a completely new road which has never before been traced out – nobody has gone there, nobody has done that! It is a beginning, a universal beginning.

So, it is an absolutely unexpected and unpredictable adventure.

There are people who love adventure. It is these I call, and I tell them this: "I invite you to the great adventure."

It is not a question of repeating spiritually what others have done before us, for our adventure begins beyond that. It is a question of a new creation, entirely new, with all the unforeseen events, the risks, the hazards it entails – a real adventure, whose goal is certain victory, but the road to which is unknown and must be traced out step by step in the unexplored. Something that has never been in this present universe and that will never be again in the same way. If that interests you... well, let us embark. What will happen to you tomorrow – I have no idea.

One must put aside all that has been foreseen, all that has been devised, all that has been constructed, and then... set off walking into the unknown.

And – come what may! There.

The Mother

The Mother on 21 February 1968

Auroville town plan

Essentially, 1965 was the year when The Mother first began to concentrate her energies and force on the project of Auroville, making mention of her intention to build, north of Pondicherry, a "universal town where men and women of all countries are able to live in peace and progressive harmony, above all creeds, all politics and all nationalities. The purpose … is to realise human unity."

As a first move she invited French architect Roger Anger (1923-2008), then living in Paris, but who had been a regular visitor to Pondicherry and the Ashram since 1957, to come up with a conceptual town plan, based on this simple sketch that she had drawn.

In handing over this sketch the only details she gave were that at the centre of the town there would

be a "Park of Unity", and that at the centre of this park there would be a building she called at first a "Pavilion of Truth", or "Pavilion of [Divine] Love", or "Pavilion of the Mother". Eventually she named it "Matrimandir", which – despite its literal translation in Sanskrit as "Temple of The Mother" – she translated in English as "The Mother's Shrine". She added that the "Park of Unity" would consist of twelve gardens representing the "twelve attributes of the (Divine) Mother", and that eventually the Matrimandir and its Park of Unity would be surrounded by a lake.

The first printed record of the word "Matrimandir (Mother's Shrine)" is found in a brochure depicting the spiral nebula model (see below), which was published in 1966 and sent to all UNESCO delegations prior to their "General Conference" of October-November 1966. It is

The original 'Galaxy' town plan

at this General Conference that UNESCO passed its first resolution in support of Auroville.

Siting of the township

As at 1965 there was still some doubt as to precisely where Auroville would be located, because one of the first possibilities was that it might be as far away as Hyderabad, where a substantial area of land had been offered. However, this offer was rejected on the grounds that there would have been certain conditions imposed. The next possibility was a site close to Ousteri Lake, north-west of Pondicherry, but as part of the Pondicherry-Tindivanam highway would have been passing through the periphery of the township this was also rejected.

Around March/April 1967, with the site for Auroville still not chosen, Roger Anger, the architect whom the Mother had asked to design the future town, brought her a map of the area north of Pondicherry. She was in her room at the Ashram and had never set foot in that area herself, not least because at the time there was no motorable road leading to it. She concentrated, and pointed to a particular location on the map, suggesting that it could be the centre of the town.

The architect took a jeep and drove to the area she had pointed at, and found there a solitary banyan tree in an almost totally barren plateau overlooking the Bay of Bengal. When he returned and informed the Mother, she was very happy about the presence of the tree, banyans being one of the seven sacred trees of India, and decided to make it Auroville's geographical centre.

Meanwhile the SAS were busy generating funds and support for the project, and planning ahead for

A lonely Palmyra tree, a sandy road, and behind an almost bare landscape.

its inauguration in 1968. An initial key step was to obtain the support of the Government of India, which they succeeded in doing in 1966. The Government's representative to UNESCO then put the project before the General Assembly of UNESCO, who that same year unanimously endorsed it as a project of importance to humanity, and passed the first of what to date have been 4 unanimous resolutions in support, the other three being in 1968, 1970 and 1983, essentially inviting "member states and international non-governmental organisations to participate in the development of Auroville as an international cultural township designed to bring together the values of different cultures and civilizations in a harmonious environment with integrated living standards which correspond to man's physical and spiritual needs."

Ah, now let's get down to work...

Do you know what we have to do?... We have to prepare Auroville's "Charter"! They will put it into the earth; when they throw in the earth from every country, they will put a metal box with the Charter in it, written on a piece of parchment. So we have to write it down.... I have a few little ideas...

(Mother unrolls a big parchment on her windowsill, facing the Samadhi. Perched on a low stool and armed with a huge black felt-pen that draws cuneiform-like letters, she starts copying Auroville's Charter while commenting on it.)

The early Banyan tree

1. Auroville belongs to nobody in particular. Auroville belongs to humanity as a whole....

So this is the material fact. Auroville belongs . . . I didn't put "to no nation" because India would have been furious. I put "belongs to nobody"—"nobody" is a vague term which I used precisely so as not to say "to no human being" or "to no nation." And I put "Auroville belongs to humanity AS A WHOLE" because it amounts to nothing! Since people can't agree together, the thing is impossible! I did it deliberately.

Then I don't say anything about "citizens" and all that, I say:

But to live in Auroville one must be a willing servitor of the Divine Consciousness.

They will all balk at "Divine," but I don't care! You understand, it's the explanation of the Matrimandir at the centre. The Matrimandir represents the Divine Consciousness. All that goes unsaid, but it's like that.

Then:

2. Auroville will be the place of an unending education, of constant progress, and a youth that never ages.

And then:

3. Auroville wants to be the bridge between the past and the future. Taking advantage of all discoveries...

All discoveries, that is, philosophical, spiritual, moral, scientific, everything—taking advantage of the past.

...of all discoveries from without and from within, Auroville will boldly spring towards future realisations.

And finally, there are two versions: "4. Auroville will be a site of research for knowledge and means of existence leading to a human unity based on mutual understanding and goodwill."

On another piece of paper, we have, "To give a living body to an actual human Unity."

So we'll alter a little.

4. Auroville will be a site of material and spiritual researches for a living embodiment of an actual Human Unity.

There.

(Mother steps down from her stool)

It's not me who wrote all this.... I noticed something so interesting: when it comes it's imperative, there's no room for arguing; I write it down—whatever I may be doing I am FORCED to write it down. But when it's not there, it's just not there! Even if I try to remember, nothing comes, it's not there! So it's clear that it doesn't come from here: it comes from somewhere above.

The Mother

28. 2. 68

Charte d'Auroville

1) Auroville n'appartient à personne en particulier. Auroville appartient à toute l'humanité dans son ensemble.

Mais pour séjourner à Auroville, il faut être le serviteur volontaire de la Conscience Divine

*

2) Auroville sera le lieu de l'éducation perpétuelle, du progrès constant et d'une jeunesse qui ne vieillit point.

*

3)   Auroville veut être le pont entre le passé et l'avenir.

Profitant de toutes les découvertes extérieures et intérieures, elle veut hardiment s'élancer vers les réalisations futures.

*

4)   Auroville sera le lieu des recherches matérielles et spirituelles pour donner un corps vivant à une unité humaine concrète.

Beauty of the new creation
(Beauty of Auroville)
The new creation strives
to better manifest the Divine.

Power of spiritual beauty
(Spiritual beauty of Auroville)
Spiritual beauty has a
contagious power.

The Mother on Auroville

Then I have written something else….They wanted to prepare a sort of brochure on Auroville to distribute to the press, the government, etc, on the 28th, and before that there is in Delhi in two or three days a conference of all nations…

So then I asked, I concentrated to know what had to be said. And all of a sudden, Sri Aurobindo gave me a revelation. That was something interesting. I concentrated to know the why, the how and so on, and all of a sudden Sri Aurobindo said ... (Mother reads out a note.)

"India has become...
It was the vision of the thing, and it instantly translated into French words

India has become the symbolic representation of all the difficulties of modern mankind.

India will be the land of its resurrection – the resurrection to a higher and truer life."

And the clear vision: the same thing which in the history of the universe made the earth the symbolic representation of the universe so as to concentrate the work on one point, the same phenomenon is now taking place: India is the representation of all human difficulties on earth, and it is in India that the . . . cure will be found. And then, that is why – **THAT IS WHY** I was made to start Auroville.

Buses and cars driving on sandy roads to Auroville's inauguration.

It came and it was so clear, so tremendously powerful! It was very interesting. It remained the whole time, for more than an hour, such a strong and clear vision, as if suddenly everything became clear. I often used to wonder about it (not "wonder," but there was a tension to understand why things, here in India, have become such a chaos, with such sordid difficulties, and all of it piling up), and instantly, everything became clear, like that. It was really interesting. And immediately there was: "Here is why you have made Auroville."

I didn't know it, you understand, I did the thing under pressure, and it took larger and larger proportions (it's becoming really worldwide), and I would wonder why. . . For a time I thought it was the only present possibility to prevent a war, but it seemed to me a somewhat superficial explanation. Then it came all of a sudden: "Ah! That's why."

And as that whole power was in it, I said, "Put it." We'll see – they won't understand anything, but that doesn't matter, it will act.

February 3, 1968, Mother's Agenda

Car park in Auroville on 28 February 1968

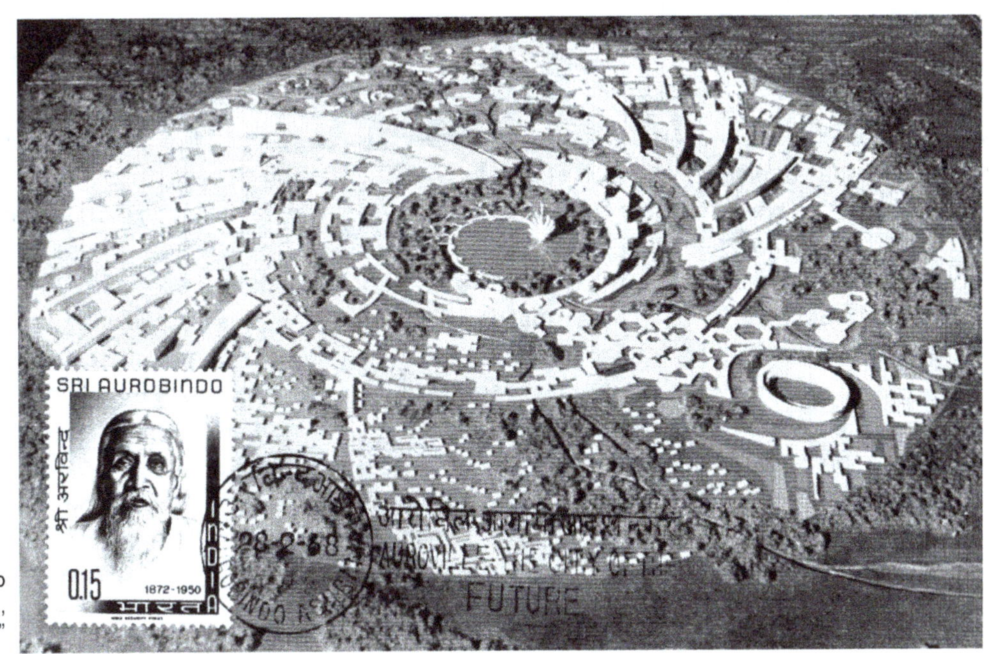

Release of a special postal stamp
on 28.2.1968,
"Auroville - The City of Future"

Nata remembers

Already from July 1967, I was, by the Mother's wish, in charge of the work of Auroville and I was directly engaged in the ongoing construction of what was meant to be a hotel, but which became first a maternity clinic, and finally, a residential building. It was the first area of work in Auroville. "Promesse" was the name Mother had given this community. It was to be a promise.

My life had undergone a sudden transplantation. From the quiet of my home, from the long hours of meditation, from the work of translating the works of Sri Aurobindo and the Mother into Italian, from the correspondence with the disciples of Mother and Sri Aurobindo spread over Italy and Spanish speaking regions, I found myself suddenly thrown back into my old work on a construction site. My vital being bounced back and, in a certain sense, and within certain limits, I became once again, for the sake of the work to be done, what I had been formerly: authoritative, accustomed to being obeyed, intolerant of mistakes, imposing my will without giving in, sometimes harsh, sometimes gentle.

That is how it was till the work began for the foundation ceremony of Auroville. There I found my true consciousness again, the yogic consciousness, I worked with a greater inner calm and greater intensity, fully conscious of the importance of the work. The one thing that troubled me was a boil on the right foot and a sense of constant tiredness. When, in the evening, I returned home around 10 o'clock, after a bath during which flowed rivers of red sand, the colour of the soil of Auroville, I sat down for dinner, I ended up falling

asleep with my head on my folded arm. At 4 o'clock in the morning, I would walk down to the Ashram for a brief meditation, to offer to the Divine the work of the day that was beginning; I would then return home and have breakfast – biscuits and very strong coffee. Immediately after that, I would get into my car to go to Auroville.

When, towards 5 o'clock, I came to the straight road that led to the place of work, my eyes caught the light of the work site. The work went on 24 hours, with 8-hour shifts. We had taken on rent about seventy 'petromax' lamps, each one as bright as a 500 watt bulb.

It was the month of February, and at that time of the morning the freshness was delightful. The work began on the 1st of February 1968 and had to be completed by the 26th, because the foundation ceremony had been fixed for the morning of the 28th.

Without going into the technical details, I will just say that the work which was completed in 25 days would normally have required 6 months for skilled workers working 8 hours a day.

The work involved the construction of an amphitheatre with a diameter of 150 metres, and around it, space for 10,000 persons sitting on mats, on the ground, and stands and steps for 2,000 persons. Towards the south-east of the centre of the amphitheatre rose a mound of about 6 metres high on which was an Urn which would contain the earth from all the countries of the world. And there had to be adequate sanitary arrangements as well as provision for drinking water.

I was told on 31st January that the ceremony for the foundation of Auroville would be held on the 28th of February and that the work should be over 2 days

earlier. I immediately went to the Mother, carrying in my hand a kind of sketch which was the only documentation provided, and I told Her that the next morning I would be on the site to begin the work, but that I could not guarantee that the work would be completed by the date already fixed. She looked into my eyes and said, "Begin the work, and do not worry about anything else."

It was like the Biblical story of the loaves and fishes. I chalked out the work on site, distributed it to the different groups, nominated the leaders of the groups, raised my eyes to heaven and said, "Mother, it is now up to you." In reality, I was only the instrument; She was the one who used it. I understood then from where came the tremendous strength which pervaded me, and the reason for the ease with which all the obstacles could be overcome.

Difficulties there were, and numerous, but all of them were resolved as if by a magic charm. There were sabotages, attempts at strikes, discussions with the Municipal authorities of the neighbouring village, with the owners of the land, with the transporters; there was delay in the arrival of consignments of the materials for the construction, etc. But on the 25th of February, that is 3 days before the scheduled date of the ceremony, everything was ready, including 8 km of road, 1.5 km of water pipes, and a parking space for 300 cars.

Preparation work for the inauguration

The construction of the stands had been planned with wood in mind, for reasons of economy, and the material was to be procured from the forest region of Kerala, with the contractor promising to deliver the

Roger Anger and Nata supervising preparation of the centre space exhibition, under the Banyan tree.

44

goods within one week of placing the order. I waited 10 days, and then saw that the wood still did not come. I stopped waiting, and began the construction in brick. On the 25th February, at the end of the work, the cement that held the bricks together was still fresh!

Something interesting happened that is worth narrating.

When I first came to the place of work, I found myself in front of an Indian landscape stretching till the horizon, without a trace of any habitation, and only a solitary Banyan tree providing some shade. I had heard a mason who knew a bit of English say that it was a sacred tree; but given the fact that in India almost all things are sacred, I thought that I would not be offending the tree, and sat down in its shade. In the succeeding days the workers began to hang their water bottles, bags and small pots and bundles from the branches of the tree. Then, one day, during one of my meetings with the Mother I was told that the spirit of the Banyan tree had come to the Mother and had complained to Her about the pain that was being inflicted on it. This was to be remedied immediately.

The next morning I made a close inspection and saw that, unfortunately, the poor Banyan tree had cause for complaint: a large number of nails had been driven into the trunk of the tree on which to hang the workers' victuals. I had the nails removed, the wounds attended to, and I explicitly prohibited everyone from coming close to the trunk of the tree. Enjoy the shade, and that was all. I believe the Banyan was satisfied, because no sooner would I sit in its shade than all the small and great worries, the pressure of the work, all lost their

The early Banyan tree and excavation work for the Amphitheatre.

force and nearly disappeared. A great peace descended upon me.

The morning of 28th February came, and as usual, at 5 o'clock, I was on the site, to ascertain that the work of watering of the roads had been carried out properly throughout the night, to lessen the inevitable dust that would be raised by the traffic on a non-asphalted road during this very dry time of the year. Everything was in order, and I had nothing to do but wait for the first vehicles to come. I did not have to wait long. At about 6, a long column of buses began to arrive, emptying itself of the first batch of people, only to go back in order to fetch more people. Very soon arrived the first cars and more buses. I do not know who made the calculation, but someone spoke of 20,000 persons, that is, 7,000 more than we had planned for.

A wave of terror invaded me when I saw the stands as if taken by assault, and occupied even by those who were not meant to be there, and what was meant for one person was now occupied by bunches of humanity who were in the lightly constructed raised area with palm leaf covering to shelter those sitting on the flight of steps from the strong rays of the sun. The thought of the still-wet cement, unable to support this excessive load, made me attempt to restrain this assault by shouting out instructions that must have seemed incoherent, because the people looked at me blankly, without making the least effort to come down from the places they were occupying. I understood that it was impossible to check the tide. I calmed down, raised my eyes to heaven and addressed to the Mother a brief prayer, "Mother, the moment has come to perform a miracle; See to it that

Eckhard Karnasch (second from left) and Nata (centre) at the Amphitheatre under construction.

all holds together, and that on this most important day for Humanity, no incident mars the occasion. Amen." And the miracle did occur. Not one brick moved, not one support gave way. The doctor at the medical centre spoke to me of only one case of stomach ache. Each and every service functioned to perfection.

Around 10.30, as if surging from the sky, the Mother's voice resounded in the air, transmitted by telephone cable directly to the loudspeakers placed all around the amphitheatre.

Greetings from Auroville to all men of good will.

Are invited to Auroville all those who thirst for progress and aspire to a higher and truer life.

Instantly, all was saturated with the presence of the Mother. It was a presence so tangible, so powerful, so direct that a wave of emotion took hold of all who were present. I have seen many Darshans, have been to see the Mother hundreds of times, but a force so intense, so prodigious, I had never felt, not even when, kneeling at Her feet, I placed my head on Her knees. It was beyond doubt that She was there, permeating with Her consciousness the human beings, the animals, the very soil which we felt was receptive.

All around were eyes moist with tears, mine included.

These words were followed by the reading of the Charter of Auroville:

Auroville belongs to nobody in particular. Auroville belongs to humanity as a whole. But to live in Auroville one must be the willing servitor of the Divine Consciousness.

Excavation work for the Amphitheatre

Auroville will be the place of an unending education, of constant progress, and a youth that never ages.

Auroville wants to be the bridge between the past and the future. Taking advantage of all discoveries from without and from within, Auroville will boldly spring towards future realisations.

Auroville will be a site of material and spiritual researches for a living embodiment of an actual human unity.

These words were followed by the most absolute silence. It seemed that all hearts were immersed in the grandeur of these words.

Suddenly, from one part of the amphitheatre, one saw arriving two youths, brother and sister, Vijay and Kiran, beautiful and pure like two young gods, carrying the white banner with the Mother's symbol and the earth from the Samadhi of Sri Aurobindo, to pour it first in the Urn prepared to receive the soil from all the countries of the world. Italy was represented by Bruno Petris and Elena Bellotti. The soil came from Sienna and had been sent by Professor Giulio Cogni.

The procession went on for several hours, at the end of which, Nolini, the oldest and most venerable disciple – he had been imprisoned with Sri Aurobindo in the Alipore jail before 1910 – closed and sealed the Urn. Thus ended the ceremony.

In the afternoon, I saw the Mother, and found Her silent and strongly indrawn. She caressed my head, gave me some flowers and said, "I knew you would do it."

I have been in the Ashram for 16 years, and even today, when I am asked which is the highest level that my consciousness has experienced, I will not hesitate and will reply, "The day of the Foundation of Auroville."

The earth road leading to the Amphitheatre.

Meera Patnaik remembers

BHUBANESWAR – November 1967 – almost 48 years ago as I write, but I can distinctly recall the porch of our beautiful bungalow in the heart of the upbeat Forest Park area of the capital, and distinctly remember hearing my father cajoling my mother to accompany him on an official trip to Bangalore, and thereafter a visit to Pondicherry and back to Bhubaneswar. Apparently all the persuasion didn't work – she declined, and said: "why not Meera?" So I was in – wow!! I was elated with joy, and excited with the thought of my first trip to Pondicherry.

That I was nominated – was it a greater divine design? Wow!

On arrival in Pondicherry we headed for the Ashram, and after paying our respects at the Samadhi we wasted no time in making a bee-line to meet The Mother. Well, apparently, without any prior appointment and on non-darshan days, no-one was permitted. Champaklalji, the Mother's attendant, made it abunduntly clear that we would not be allowed in.

It was then that my father, in his typical commanding tenor voice, told Champaklalji that "I have come to meet my Mother and I don't need any permission to meet Her." Apparently she heard the commotion, and to our utter delight we were waved in up to Her room.

I was just ecstatic. We entered Her chamber, and lo and behold – such humble and yet pristine and serene settings – and there sat this gracious lady looking ever so beautiful at her desk, with pen in hand. Electrifying. My heart started pounding in ecstasy, and with tears rolling down my cheeks I kneeled in front of

Carrying the soil from Orissa

her and bowed down to kiss the "lotus feet" in divine reverence.

As I looked at her, she looked straight into my eyes and I just stood motionless – not for a moment wanting to move away from such a divine omni-presence and with the sole wish to just lean on her for always! Her gaze gently withdrew from mine, which was unwavering, to that of a beautiful rose bloom. She gently handed me the red rose, smiled, and then we had to leave. Instantly, I became conscious of the Mother's invisible seal on my soul!

This was the formative period when the Mother's dream of a universal city was being discussed and programmed. A place which no nation could claim as its own and where humans with sincere aspirations could live freely as citizens of the world and obey "one single authority, that of the supreme truth, a place of peace concord and harmony…,"

My father and I went to meet Navajatji after the darshan and observed that discussions and preparations were on for the inauguration ceremony of Auroville. He spoke to my father regarding participation of the State of Orissa. Then, looking at me, he said: "let Meera represent Orissa".

I just couldn't believe what I had just heard – me, as an invited guest of the Mother! Overwhelmed with gratitude, and in all humility, I mentally bowed at Her lotus feet.

BHUBANESWAR – 27th February 1968, and the day had dawned to realise my dreams. Who would have imagined that I would be a "chosen" one, along with the son of the Speaker of the Orissa Legislative Assembly, to represent Orissa. We arrived in Pondicherry with the soil of the State for amalgamation with the soil brought by teenager representatives of over 120 nations and other states of India.

Airlines the world over, including Indian Airlines, had offered free passage and return for this event, to ensure participation of national representatives from across the globe. On our flight from Calcutta to Madras itself, there were lots of children from different parts of the world. It was a multi-lingual, multi-coloured mass of happy teenagers. Shy as I was then, there was the initial reluctance to mingle, but before long the atmosphere was so beautiful; it was as if all were friends already since long!

Smiling faces, introductory embraces, greetings in their respective languages, and one could see smiling faces and goodwill flowing everywhere.

MADRAS – 27th February 1968. On landing at Madras, we were greeted by volunteers wearing Auroville badges, with a welcome smile and warmth.

Yes, I was miles away from home and family, but so 'at home' with Mother's family. All the fear and apprehensions I had at the time of boarding the flight were by now dispelled, with a consciousness of confidence as Mother's child.

The journey from Madras to Pondicherry was by bus, and camaraderie and fun accompanied our journey. A guitarist began strumming and all went into singing mode. Wow – I was enjoying the fun, and something; I had never ever felt so free and happy! The atmosphere was charged with a divine presence.

PONDICHERRY – 27th February 1968. On arrival at Pondicherry we were again greeted by volunteers with a smile and such warmth. We were then briefed as to our boarding and lodging arrangements and the programme. At this juncture one of the volunteers, Jhumur di, an ashramite, took my hand and said to her companion "ami eke badi neeye jabo" (I want to take her home). She picked up my suitcase and we walked to her home, where on reaching she yelled out to her mother and said, "dekho, ke eseche" (look who's here). The lady, with a very pleasant disposition, welcomed me into their home, and it is there I stayed, with loads of love and affection showered on me. It was home away from home. It was as if I had surrendered to the divine intervention, for today when viewed in retrospect every detail of my visit was meticulously taken care of. It was all Her plan!

The programme for the Inauguration was charted out under the personal direction and guidance of the Mother. Leaflets of the ceremonies and time details were provided along with identification badges to all national and international representatives.

AUROVILLE – 28th February 1968. We were all assembled in a vast open space with just a Banyan tree standing majestically in an area which was otherwise just

Invitation card for the Auroville inauguration.

Godhead
Pure and perfect,
puts forth its force in the world.

**Firmness of the new creation
(Firmness of Auroville)**
The new creation wants
to be steadfast
in its manifestation.

acres of barren land, and in the centre of which was the historic marble Lotus Urn artistically designed to take the soil of all the participating nations. This area was later to be developed into the Auroville Amphitheatre, with a proposed majestic Matrimandir adjacent surrounded by manicured gardens and water bodies.

Sitting in anticipation of the ceremonies to begin I couldn't help but wonder at the very thought that here was I - AS A GUEST OF THE MOTHER – OF THE DIVINE. Who could be luckier than me! It was awesome.

28/2/1968 – 10.30hrs – the Mother's voice was heard emanating from her room in Pondicherry, and this certainly electrified the entire congregation assembled there to witness the birth of her dream – The City of Auroville.

The Mother spoke in French: "Greetings from Auroville to all men of goodwill. Invited to Auroville – are those who thirst for progress and aspire to a higher and truer life". After a brief pause, the area was engulfed in silence, as she spoke again in French and English proclaiming the historic Charter for the city. The Charter was read out in various languages of the representative nations, while the filling of the beautiful lotus Urn commenced. The teams (a boy and girl) from different nations carried the flag and soil of their land, ceremoniously dropping it into the Urn, to symbolise world unity.

The first at the Urn were the ashramite combo of Vijay bhai and Kiran didi, then followed by other nations in alphabetical order. When it was our tUrn to parade up the ramp to the Urn, I was still in a daze! Was it all really happening, the whole world watching, and a humble me being part of this great event? The feeling within me was difficult to express in words. A grand spectacle, accompanied by soft musical strings, and thunderous applause as I reached the Urn from the Orissa camp of onlookers. As we came down the ramp, we were directed to a huge cloth scroll where each participant signed in their respective languages.

Thereafter, each one of us was presented with a lotus flower – a gift from the divine Mother. A gift most precious which I have preserved and cherish to date. Mother – you made us feel so very special!

After the main ceremony was over, we were invited over for lunch organised by Navajatji, the General Secretary of the Sri Aurobindo Society. We were overwhelmed by the warm reception and the excellent spread for lunch. In fact wherever we went the reception we got was warm and friendly.

Post lunch, there was an informal meeting held in the library premises in the presence of the Deputy Director General of UNESCO, and an opportunity given to all to clear any doubts we may have had. There were lots of questions and answers in a very invigorating session. Personally I never did have any doubts whatsoever: who could doubt what can be termed as a Divine Creation! I just silently listened and prayed to make me an instrument in Her divine work.

In the evening we all assembled in the Society House. Each one of us was presented with a perfume made and bottled and beautifully packed by the Ashramites. It carried the label of Auroville. We were also presented with a beautiful handkerchief which carried the symbol of Auroville.

A special dinner was laid out for all of us. Of course then came the sad time to say goodbye. Exchanging addresses, hugs and emotional scenes followed, bidding adieu!

Strange indeed it was, considering that we were together for just two days and the extent of bonhomie and friendship that developed. An emotional farewell no doubt, but I could not help but wonder at Her play – set out proving how citizens of the world can live together in harmony, in love, irrespective of their colour, religion or language, or which country they came from.

29th of February – 10.00hrs – Most of the participants had left. I however stayed back for Balcony Darshan – a picture that will always remain vividly etched in my mind. A period in time which I will cherish for ever.

My parting words were… "Bye, bye Auroville – I will be back to see you grow!"

I was fortunate to see Auroville grow year on year and participate in the construction of the now strikingly beautiful edifice – The Matrmandir. A zone for meditation, as clean and pure as they come.

Although I do not stay in Auroville, I do consider myself AUROVILIAN.

With reverence, I remain bowed, seeking her noble hand of guidance through the vicissitudes of life.

The Auroville Experience

The Plan of Auroville
Mona Sarkar's conversations with The Mother

Have you seen the plan of Auroville?

Yes, Mother.

Is it not magnificent? Do you like it?

Yes, Mother, very much.

It is really beautiful.

Yes, Mother. It is going to be an enormous lot of work.

Mona Sarkar's conversations with The Mother, 27.3.66

About the Inauguration Ceremony

Good morning.

Good morning, Sweet Mother.

. . . Now, let us see, somebody has asked me to tell you . . . No, it was I who said that I would talk to you when you come on Sunday.

You know what will take place there, in Auroville, on the 28th. It will be the inauguration. We will need you on that day. Actually, it is I who proposed your name. It will be around 10 or10.30, something like that. We will have the ceremony and the people will be assembled to see it

Jean Maslow discussing about the arrangements with Mona Sarkar.

and it is then that we will need you, only on the 28th. You know, we have distributed the work among many persons so that everything happens as it should and each one does his work.

When Roger [*the Auroville architect*] asked me for someone who would organise things on the spot and manage the crowd which will come to see the function, because it is necessary that everyone is treated properly and all remain in their allotted places, I immediately thought of you. I said that we could give this responsibility to Mona. He will be the best person, because I know that he has organised many things of this kind. I believe that if he takes it up, he will be able to do it. We can depend on him, he is the only one for organising this kind of work.

Do you remember, you had organised night watches and also the work in the rice fields? You remember, you had organised things on different occasions with your boys? It will be something similar, if you do it in Auroville too.

I am sorry, but I put your name without asking you. I do not know whether you will accept this work or not. As soon as I was told this, I proposed your name because I believed you would be the best person to manage a crowd like this. If you do it, Roger will be very happy, and me too.

Mother, there is no question when it is You who ask me.

It is good my child, it will be only on 28th at the time of inauguration and only in the morning. We will require you with fifty of your boys. Will you be able to get fifty boys?

Yes, Mother.

I do not think we will need fifty boys; but how many can you get?

As many as I am asked to get.

You know, we will request the police to control the crowd, but I said it would be better that Mona with his boys takes care of it. It is expected that there will be a crowd of 10,000 people for the ceremony, but I do not believe that we will have so many people. I think that there might be just half of that, around 5,000 people. And for all those people, it is necessary that you take care of them, making them go where they need to be, each in his place, and everything well organised. It

should not be that these people hang around where they should not, in the forum or among the children who will be participating in the ceremony. No, everyone must be in their respective places, without any disorder. It is this that you should see to and organise.

And then there will be also a big crowd of the villagers who live close by. Naturally, they will come to see what is happening. All this must be well organised.

Mother, for the people from the villages, it would be better if the police looked after them.

Yes, that is better and you will take care of the other crowd.

But there will be no barriers made with ropes to prevent the people. That is why one must be careful that the people don't walk about all over the place.

But how many boys can you get? How many?

As many as you want, Mother.

No, I mean whenever you do something like this and you need boys, how many do you get?

It depends.

Similarly, if you call them now, how many will be at your disposal?

Yes, I can find fifty boys.

Oh! Can you get fifty boys?

Yes, Mother; but if there are classes on that day, it will be a little difficult.

No, there will be no school that day. Everything will be closed. It will be a holiday.

Then, it is not difficult.

I do not know, perhaps there will be no games [*physical education activities*], nothing in the afternoon too. In any case, it doesn't make any difference whether there is something in the afternoon or not because it is in the morning that we will have the ceremony. And there will be no school. But I do not think we will need fifty persons. Then you can easily get fifty boys, can you?

Yes, Mother.

It's good. Do you know what exactly we will do for the ceremony? There will be the central area with the Urn and all that, where the children aged 14 to 18 who have come from each country for the ceremony will assemble. They will be around 200 if all of them come.

It is they who will be performing the ceremony. That is why they will be very close to the Urn, to one side. And then, there will be a pavilion for the important people who will come.

You mean, the invitees?

Yes, the invitees who will be in the pavilion meant for them; you don't have to bother about them, because there will be others who will take care of them, who will lead them to their seats in some order, I don't quite know, according to their position. But that is not your concern. You, you must, with your volunteers, deal with the whole crowd which will be there to witness the ceremony. They will need to be accommodated properly, where they should be. Each in his place. This must be organised in a disciplined way, so that the people do not walk about during the ceremony, coming in where they shouldn't be. To control them, and put them in their proper area, all that is what you will have to organise well with your boys.

Yes, Mother.

And then, there will also be the villagers – eager to know what is happening – creeping into the central area. That would be catastrophic! This must be prevented, and they will need to be kept in their allotted places. All this must be in order. That is your work.

Yes, Mother, but the police should take care of the villagers. It is better if the police do it.

Yes, I too think so. Well, you will see to all this.

It will be only for the morning, and you know how to do it. You have a lot of experience. You do this often, don't you?

No, Mother, nowadays it is Ajit who looks after everything, controlling the crowd during Darshan. . .

Oh! I didn't know that. You are not doing it anymore?

No, Mother. It is he who is doing all this; but if you want me to do it, I will do it.

I didn't know that; I thought you were looking after all this. And if I had known it before, I would have talked to Ajit. It was just yesterday that he came to see me for his Birthday. If I had known this before. . . . But I thought that it was you who were in charge of all this. That is why I remembered you, and I proposed your name.

Now, if you do it, it will be good; or if you want somebody else to do it. . . as you wish, my child.

When You have asked me to do it, I will do it, but I will ask Ajit and the others to help me.

Yes, my child, it is better like that. You will see that everything happens in an orderly manner and in harmony.

I do not know how many persons will be there that day, but in any case you will be ready with the boys. It is good. So you can talk to Roger to know what will be the best for all and you can also get to know the details of the ceremony and all that, how it will be conducted. . . Anyway, you know Roger.

Yes, Mother.

Do you meet him from time to time?

Yes, Mother.

Well, see him, and it is he who will tell you what has to be done. Good. Well, arrange all this with the boys.

(After a while)

But let us see . . . it would be a good idea if we had something like a badge, so that one could distinguish the volunteers. Yes, I will talk to Roger to make a sort of badge for the volunteers. It is a good idea.

Buses waiting in Pondicherry for transporting people to Auroville.

(Mother shows me a flower)

You know this? It is the flower of Auroville ('Godhead'[1]). We can have something like this to wear on the chest.

Not the flower, but a print, we pin it up and put it here *(the chest)*. All of you will be smart with it, and we will easily be able to distinguish who is a volunteer. Yes, I will tell him this so that the badges are made. It is good. You will all be magnificent with it, on the chest. Well, it's decided, because I told them that I would talk to Mona when I see him on Sunday. And it is I who have proposed your name. No-one else. I told them

____

1 *Hibiscus rosa-sinensis 'Cromwell'*

that he would be the best person if he did this work. And I have put you as – what do we say . . . *(Mother looks at the papers)* yes, yes, Chief of Public Security. You understand?

Yes, Mother.

To organise for the safety of the public. It's good like this; one work is done, and I am sure that it is in responsible hands.

You will do it very well, there is no doubt. That is all.

Mona Sarkar's conversations with The Mother, *28.1.68*
(These conversations were not recorded on any device, but written out from memory)

Kiran Poddar holding Mother's flag.

The Inauguration Day, 28 February 1968

Mona Sarkar's conversations with The Mother

[Two children, a boy and a girl, representing the different countries of the world were to place the soil of their country in the lotus-bud-shaped Urn at the centre of Auroville during the inauguration ceremony. Vijay and Kiran Poddar had been chosen by the Mother to carry the sand from the Samadhi for placing it in the Urn. In their discussion, among other things, the question of dress also arose. What should they wear? The question was referred to the Mother for her decision.]

If they ask me, I will tell them to wear what they wear every day.

Even the people who will be there for the ceremony, will come in their own way. I do not insist that they be dressed the way we want them, because these things have no value even for those who will be there to see the ceremony.

There are always people of good will who, moreover, are few, but when they watch the ceremony, they will always see the good side of what is happening. They see only the best things that emerge. Their attention will be drawn to the beauty and the harmony. And they will say, "It was beautiful, all that!" because they have a heart which responds to what is beautiful. They do not at all see if there was a bad side in all that. These are the people of goodwill.

And then there are others who from the beginning will see only the bad side of things. They come with the idea that nothing is working properly. And they will only see the disharmony and uselessness of things. They will

Vijay Poddar signs the scroll.

always look with an eye to find faults, to give a bad twist to things, to see wrongly, even when one does the best possible. For them, it will always be something humdrum or bad. They can never appreciate things done well, because they always have a bad attitude. That is why they see only the bad.

And then there are others who are indifferent, who will say nothing, because it is all the same to them whatever happens.

That is why I do not give any importance to what these people say. The opinion of these people has no value, because we will always find the three categories of people in a crowd like that.

You can speak to Kiran and Vijay and tell them that they can put on what they want. It is not the outward appearance that counts; the important thing is the inner attitude.

If they try to purify themselves, to become conscious of what is happening, to open to the force which is working, to aspire, to be ready, to become sincere to act as one should, to be conscious always of that (gesture indicating the heart), and all that, to do things in a way that helps them to become more conscious . . . in short, they must feel and try to participate as much as possible in what is being done in Auroville – to open to the consciousness and widen oneself to receive it...

The attitude that is needed, to call the consciousness, to purify the thought, to become ready to give oneself entirely . . . To think of the Creative Force of the Supreme which is at work in Auroville. . . to become ready to receive what is happening in Auroville, to become conscious of what I have been assigned to do.

And to remember that it would have been I who would have done that instead of these children. It is because I do not come out, that these children are replacing me. To feel that it is I who shall be pouring the soil instead of them. It is this which is important. The important thing is to prepare oneself inwardly.

Moreover, they have written to me a beautiful letter telling me what they want to do on that day and asking me how I want it to be done. I am very happy to have read that sweet letter. They have understood what is to be done, and the attitude is very good and right. I know how they will do it. I am sure that they will do exactly as I want.

That is why I have chosen these children to represent me. There is no doubt that I have chosen well. They are good. I have all the confidence in them and they will do exactly as I want. Exactly as it should be done. They will be my representatives. I have confidence that they are worthy of the work.

I have called Vijay and Kiran on the 28th. They will come to meet me at about 8.00 in the morning. I will give them the Charter which I have already written and the sand from the Samadhi which is with me. They have already brought the sand from the Samadhi. I will give them all these when they come to see me. They will carry this with them there. And they will be the first to pour the sand of the Samadhi and place the Charter. And then the other countries will follow. They will be the first to pour the soil in the Urn.

I have chosen these children because they are capable of doing it as I want them to. They are preparing themselves, and I am sure that they will do it as if it is I who am doing it.

They will come to see me towards 8.00 in the morning. They will come in the same dress they will wear for the ceremony and go directly from here. You can tell them this. I am sure they will do very well.

Mona Sarkar's conversations with The Mother, 18.2.68 (These conversations were not recorded on any device, but written out from memory)

The Founding of Auroville

Mme. Yvonne Robert Gaebelé

There, where breathes the spirit — Aurovilie

On the morning of the 28th of February, 1968 the Bay of Bengal woke up powdered with gold.

The gold was colouring the roofs of the houses of Pondicherry and as the splendid orb mounted up in the sky the whole countryside around appeared to be bathing in the royal light.

It was indeed the supreme festival of the light which awaited us at the place, chosen out of all others, for the construction of Auroville.

Imagine, nor far from Pondicherry, a sort of immense arena with slopes around rising in grades, the whole wonderously arranged to receive thousands of spectators of whom several had come from great distances to participate in the ceremony of the day.

In the centre of the arena was an elevation of earth, where one could reach by a circular way to an urn with a lid styled as a lotus bud. This urn was to contain the earth from 124 countries, brought from all parts, on which the future city would be built. After the loudspeakers had called for silence, first arose the voice of the Mother who spoke from a distance from her room in the Ashram.

What was the Mother saying?... She was reading the Charter of Auroville and in the solemn silence first fell the sublime words, "Auroville belongs to nobody in particular, it belongs to humanity as a whole. But to live in Auroville one must be the willing servitor of the Divine Consciousness." This relinquishment, absolute and

Ashram volunteers assembled for coordinating the event

deliberate, contrasted so strongly, from the first, with the spirt of the century that one could not but admire and bow down before a realisation of such amplitude and serenity. Then the procession commenced.

The first pair carried the flag of the Mother, the golden wheel on the sky-blue base, symbol of the Mother's occult and transcendental powers. The two young ones appeared from the horizon, with slow steps they followed the triumphal path lined by volunteers and began to climb the symbolic cone. Soon the flag fluttered there, caressed by the wind while the young ones carefully placed the earth of the Ashram and the Charter of Auroville in the depths of the urn.

Then other pairs followed, with very slow steps, as if cadenced by a low-toned music, while the Charter was being read in the principal languages of the world. All were arriving, pair after pair, surging from the horizon, the young

girl carrying the name of the country they represented, the young boy with the soil of the country in a vessel. When they arrived at the top, near the urn, with a pious gesture the soil was poured over the other soil already sunk there, and then they came down the opposite side. Some pairs wore the costume of the country to which they belonged. Thus one could admire the colours of the rich costumes of Africa. Immense Russia was represented by two quite small infants, blond and charming. Then each state of India had its turn. No country of the world was forgotten — from the icy lands of the Pole up to those of the tiny states of the Equator. The last pair carried the orange-coloured flag of Auroville evolving with a symbolic lotus at its centre.

The silence became, if that was possible, yet profounder when was seen moving forth the noble disciple of the Ashram, Nolini, the earliest and one of the oldest, the disciple from the first days of the beloved Master, Sri Aurobindo. Accompanied by his son he came to seal the urn. When he climbed the cone and stood at the top, dressed in immaculate clothes, with his face of handsomely grave features, one could say some Vedic priest of the ancient ages was officiating at the altar, lighting there the fire of sacrifice.

Is Auroville not the altar on which must be burnt away for ever all the evil passions so that the world, grown pure, may teach the new Evangel to the earth of man?

Auroville - The City of New life

The Auroville badge

Good Morning.

Good Morning, Sweet Mother.

I have just received the badges now. They are very beautiful. There are 500 of them. You can give the badges to the volunteers so that one can distinguish them easily. They would look *chic* with it.

Mother, we have decided that the volunteers will be dressed fully in white, white trousers, white shirt and white shoes.

Yes, it is very good, and with the badge here (*on the chest*), they will be very smart. It is good. . . You can bring those things which are on the tray, wrapped in paper. They are heavy. You can bring them here. I will show them to Roger. You can call Roger now.

I don't know where he would like to keep them. There are badges for those who participate in the work. After the 28th they can keep it as a souvenir of Auroville. They can keep these badges for those who will be part of the work. It will be a gift on behalf of Auroville.

Now call Roger. *Yes, Mother.*

(*To Roger*) These are the badges for the security volunteers. Where do you want me to send them? They are heavy, Mona can take them.

(*Vasudha*) *To Roger's house, Mother, Society House, upstairs.* (*Mother to Mona*) Well, you take them there. It is heavy. *Yes, Mother.* It is all right.

Mona Sarkar's conversations with The Mother, 21.2.68
(These conversations were not recorded on any device but written out from memory)

The Inauguration Ceremony

Mother, we are preparing for the programme of the 28th February.

Is everything ready?

Not yet, Mother. But things are moving.

The pavilion and all that to accommodate the people is complete?

Yes, Mother, for the VIPs, it is ready.

Yes, it is nice, it is beautiful.

Yes, Mother, but not for the people of the Ashram.

How?

The place where people will sit, nothing has been done. They will all be in the sun.

If . . .

Mother, the shade that has been provided does not help much, because of the slope. The people will not be able to see if there is someone standing in front of them.

But who planned it?

Roger.

(Mother laughs) Everyone will be in the sun?

Yes, Mother, nearly everyone. The shelter can provide for three rows, and some area has to be demarcated for the villagers.

Yes, that needs to be done.

Today, we went with the police and they said an area has to be reserved for the villagers, otherwise it would be difficult. A cordoning off with a rope may be required.

But no place was reserved for the villagers? It is a must.

Yes, Mother, but a rope cordon will be needed.

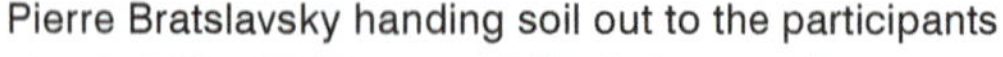
Pierre Bratslavsky handing soil out to the participants

Speak to your boys; they should behave with gentleness and tact. They should not be rude or insolent.They have to be very gentle and control well.

Mother, for the villagers, the police will be responsible, because we do not know the language and also to avoid a direct contact.

You have done well to let the police take care of that. And where will you put those who come from the Ashram?

Some in the shade, and the others in the sun. Roger does not want the people to be sitting, except in one area.

But where will the people sit?

I don't know, Mother.

But then they will see nothing . . .

I don't know. At least there is a shade for the VIP's, chairs and all that . . . but the others will be in the sun.

But then they must sit on the slope. You can tell them personally that they should bring their umbrellas, this way they will not be in the sun all the time.

Yes, Mother. But the best would be if the sky is cloudy.

Yes, that would be best, but it should not rain; that would spoil everything.

Yes, Mother, that is why we pray to you that the sky remains cloudy.

I do not see what can be done.

If you want it to be, it will be. It is our prayer to you.

We will see. It would be ideal if the sky was cloudy.

Yes, Mother, you will do what is required.

We will see.

Mona Sarkar's conversations with The Mother, 25.2.68

After the Ceremony

So, it went off well, the ceremony yesterday?

Yes, Mother, it went off very well.

Good.

Inside, the ceremony was without a flaw. All happened very well in a charged atmosphere. But outside the area, there was a considerable confusion.

What? I don't understand. Outside what? And what happened?

Outside the arena, not where the ceremony was being held. It was magnificent there. But outside . . .

So, my voice could not be heard when I read out the message?

Yes, we heard it very well. It was that which created the atmosphere. Exactly at 10:30, we heard your voice. And our children stood at attention. No one moved. The boys were in their place and it looked magnificent. And then we heard your voice. It carried us away, because the atmosphere was charged.

We knew nothing of what was happening outside. Inside it was so magnificent. Our boys did their work well.

What was happening outside?

People who were not allowed inside, they were moving about here and there and it was difficult to control them. The police did nothing.

How many people were there?

At least 1,200

1,200?

Yes, I think so. And it was very difficult to control them. But inside one was not at all aware of what was happening outside.

But the ceremony went off well?

Yes, Mother, very well.

Mona Sarkar's conversations with The Mother, 29.2.68
(These conversations were not recorded on any device,
but written out from memory)

Preparing the sign boards and flags for the entry of the delegates.

The Inauguration day

February 28, 1968

The delegates, young people from India and abroad, boarded the buses, four or five buses with hundreds of people. People came from the Sri Aurobindo Ashram, from all the Indian states and foreign countries, from all the villages around. Buses, cars and many bicycles.

From Jipmer hospital onwards there was nothing: a desert. Edayanchavadi was a sleepy village of mud huts. Only peanut fields, a few palmyra trees growing here and there in line, and not so many. One could see everything from here down to Pondicherry. Then the buses stopped in the middle of nowhere and everybody got out. It was about 10 a.m., but already very hot. Shades were put up and the delegates had to wait there. The atmosphere was vibrating. One could feel the enormity of the event; it was the human unity, the international atmosphere, like what you may feel in the Olympic Games, but there it is very much vital, while here it was bright, it was of another quality.

All the delegates, in alphabetical order, one by one had to go to the Urn in the middle of an upcoming amphitheatre and place soil of their country in the Urn. Then they had to sign a scroll.

The Auroville Charter was read out in many languages.

The Inaugural event

The entire Ashram has gone to Auroville to attend its inauguration. The ceremony, which would take 75 minutes, began at 10.24 with the white-clad announcer briefly explaining the order of events to come to the 5,000 or so people assembled in the amphitheatre. At 10.30 there was the sound of a gong, there were a few bars of Mother's music, then came Mother's voice, relayed from her room in the Ashram: Mother reads out her message, which is broadcast live to Auroville through All India Radio:

> *Salut d'Auroville à tous les hommes de bonne volonté. Sont conviés à Auroville tous ceux qui ont soif de progrès et aspirent à une vie plus haute et plus vraie.*

Greetings from Auroville to all men of good will. Are invited to Auroville all those who thirst for progress and aspire to a higher and truer life.

A few more bars of music followed, then Mother read The Charter of Auroville in French.

Auroville's Charter

1. Auroville belongs to nobody in particular. Auroville belongs to humanity as a whole.
   But to live in Auroville one must be a willing servitor of the Divine Consciousness.

2. **Auroville will be the place of an unending education, of constant progress, and a youth that never ages.**

3. **Auroville wants to be the bridge between the past and the future. Taking advantage of all discoveries from without and from within, Auroville will boldly spring towards future realisations.**

4. **Auroville will be a site of material and spiritual researches for a living embodiment of an actual Human Unity.**

(then the microphone is switched off. . . silence)

The announcer then stated, "Now the earth from the Ashram will be put in the Urn." Kiran and Vijay Poddar approached the Urn, Kiran carrying Mother's flag and Vijay carrying earth from the Samadhi and a stainless steel container with inside the scroll with The Charter of Auroville in Mother's handwriting. As they reached the Urn Sunil's 1968 New Year music began to be played, along with Mother's New Year message: "Remain young, Never stop striving towards Perfection." The stainless steel container was lowered deep into the Urn using ribbons, along with the earth.

The announcer then introduced the formula which would be followed for the rest of the ceremony. The Charter would be read successively in 16 languages by nationals (usually Ashramites) of those countries or

cultures (the languages in order were Tamil, Sanskrit, English, Arabic, Chinese, Dutch, German, Greek, Hebrew, Italian, Japanese, Norwegian, Russian, Spanish, Swedish and Tibetan). Before each reading the announcer would introduce the translation – "Now the Charter in Tamil will be read…" – and specify which states of India or countries would approach the Urn during that reading (the states first, countries afterwards, all in alphabetical order).

In all, two young delegates from each of the 23 States or Union Territories of India and representatives from 124 countries (63 persons were delegated by embassies, the rest were students from the Ashram school) walked up to the Urn. In each pair, one would carry a placard with the name of their State or country, the other would carry earth (or a substitute) from that State or country in a small bowl. After the earth was tipped into the Urn, the representatives walked down the ramp from the Urn. Their placard was taken and placed in a pre-assigned socket, they signed a scroll with their names and the name of their State or country, and then they walked up a ramp out of the central arena.

Finally came the announcement, "Now the earth of Auroville will be put in the Urn. Then the Urn will be sealed." Michel (Kalya) and Fabienne, Mother's great-grandchildren, approached the Urn. Michel carried Auroville earth while Fabienne carried the Auroville flag (the symbol was an open lotus with another lotus in its centre against a background of 'dawn gold'). Then Nolini and his son walked to the Urn. He placed the lid over the top and removed the screwed handle. The Urn was sealed, the inauguration of Auroville complete.

Mother's Agenda

Madhav Pandit reading in Sanskrit.

Theodora Karnasch reading the Auroville Charter in German.

The Mother on preparation
for 28 February 1968

I've spent all my days and all my nights quieting the atmosphere, it had taken such proportions. . . . You know, those movements which start whirling like that, like the wind in a cyclone or at sea, and it goes on whirling faster and faster, more and more strongly and forcefully. Then people fall ill, they get worn out, they can't do anything anymore. For the past three days I've spent my time calming and calming the atmosphere. Luckily they came to me (it wasn't to "me", naturally), they felt there was something stable here that could stop this disorder, otherwise. . . But it was very difficult because of the really large number of additions from outside: on the 21st, at the Darshan, they were more than four thousand people down in the street, and there are all those who came to be here today and tomorrow, so it must mean five or six thousand people to feed, accommodate . . . a whole work. Then they asked me, naturally, that it shouldn't rain, but that it shouldn't be sunny either! (Mother laughs) So it was a bit difficult, but a short while ago, Z came to tell me that Auroville's area was clouded, without sunshine... All these little entities are quite obliging, but they're asked impossible things! I get requests, "Ah, I need rain," and at the same time, "Oh, no, I don't want rain"; "Ah, I need sunshine," and "Oh, no, I don't want sunshine..." How can they manage it?

Mother's Agenda

Bottom right: Norman Dowsett from the Sri Aurobindo Society and M.P. Pandit (r).

Conversation between Mother and a disciple about Auroville on February 28, 1968

One needs to have an absolutely transparent sincerity. Lack of sincerity is at present the cause of difficulties.

Insincerity is in all men. There are perhaps a hundred totally sincere men on earth. Man's very nature is what makes him insincere. It's very complicated, for he is constantly cheating with himself, hiding the truth from himself, finding excuses for himself. Yoga is the way to become sincere in all the parts of one's being.

It is difficult to be sincere, but one can at least be mentally sincere – this is what one can demand from Aurovilians.

The Force is there, present as never before; what prevents it from descending and being felt is men's insincerity. The world is steeped in falsehood, all relationships between men have so far been based only on falsehood and deceit. Diplomacy between nations is based on falsehood. They claim they want peace and on the other hand arm themselves. A transparent sincerity in man and between nations will alone permit the coming of a transformed world.

Auroville is the first attempt in the experiment. A new world will be born if men consent to strive for transformation and the search for sincerity – it can be done. It took millennia to evolve from animal to man; today man, thanks to his mind, can accelerate things and will a transformation towards a man who will be God.

Exhibition under the Banyan tree and bus parking.

This transformation with the help of the mind, through self-analysis, is a first stage; afterwards, vital impulses must be transformed – which is far more difficult; then, most of all, the physical: each cell of our body will have to become conscious. It is the work I am doing here. It will allow the conquest of death. It's another story; that will be future mankind, perhaps in centuries, perhaps sooner. It will depend on men, on peoples.

Auroville is the first step towards this goal.

Mother's Agenda

The Banyan tree festively decorated for Auroville's Inauguration day.

Dr. Salah-El-Din Tewfik,
UNESCO's Chief of Mission,
New Delhi

Navajata, Chief Executive, Sri Aurobindo Society and Auroville (second and third from left) showing to dignitaries and other visitors the maquette of the future township.

Out of the blue

Manoj Das Gupta, trustee of the Sri Aurobindo Ashram, remembers...

I 'll try to say whatever I remember, but I do not claim any absolute authenticity as I have a very bad memory.

In January 1968 I was down with paratyphoid. I was kept to my bed for a few weeks, and one day, as I was lying in my cot, probably towards the end of January or the beginning of February, Roger Anger, Navajata and Gilbert came to visit me. They came to tell me that Mother had asked me to write the Charter of Auroville. I was taken aback. "Charter? What does it mean?" I asked. They told me, "How you conceive this township." If I remember correctly, what they said was that someone had written a draft charter or something like that, and Mother was not quite satisfied and had suggested my name. I drafted something, and when Mother's Charter was made public I was pleased to see that some of the things I had mentioned were there – a place for perpetual education, no religion, some of these things. But it is very unfortunate that I did not keep any copy of what I had sent to her.

Then – the date on the note is February 24th, but I am doubtful about that – someone had written to Mother:

Douce Mère,

It is necessary that there be one central information office for the Auroville Function where every piece of information is collected and then suitably arranged to be available to others who need it.

Pierre Bratslavsky (holding the Auroville flag), Vincenzo Maiolini and RogerAnger.

Such an office is already supposed to be in existence with Norman Oscar, but all information is not available there.

If You Yourself, Douce Mere, appoint someone to this work, it will be effectively done. Then each one will be instructed to send every piece of information small or big to this central office and also the person in charge will go round and collect the information himself.

Below it Mother had written…
Manoj will do that work.

That came out of the blue for me. On January 31st, I wrote to Mother informing Her that I had recovered and that it appeared that She had appointed me for something for Auroville, but that I had no experience. I asked Her to give me the Force and Guidance so that I could be Her worthy instrument for the Work.

Mother replied that Roger would inform me what was to be done. But then She added, in this marvellous caring way of hers, that for the moment I shouldn't fatigue myself in order that I become completely healed. "My tenderness is with you and my blessings so that you can recuperate."

I started to teach again on February 11th. A few days later, I learned that I had to replace Gilbert for his work in Auroville (he was in charge of press relations with Eckhardt) during his absence. But I also learned from Navajata that I had to take responsibility for the children who would come for the ceremony. I wrote to Mother asking Her what She expected from me.

Unfortunately I do not remember any more what She said to me when I visited Her with Roger. On 17 February I sent Mother a list of 33 countries from where earth

would arrive, to be deposited in the Urn, and a list of the countries which had agreed to send children for the ceremony. Some countries had asked that children form the Ashram school would represent them.

There were, of course, many problems of organization. For example, three persons each believed they were responsible for the planned youth conference. Mother's response is very instructive and I believe valid even today for both the Ashram and Auroville.

"Here nobody can be the exclusive leader – everybody has to learn to collaborate. It is a very good discipline for the vanity, self-love, and the excessive sense of importance of personalities...
Blessings,
Mother

On the 27th, I wrote to Mother that I understood that She had chosen me to give some souvenirs for the children, that we had decided to do that after dinner that evening, and if this was all right? It also appeared that Mona Sarkar had asked me to work with him during the ceremony, and I asked Her if that was OK as I was free that day. Mother replied that it was OK. The youth camp took place at the Sri Aurobindo Society office, after the dinner. I do not remember anymore what the gifts were.

The atmosphere during the ceremony? A tremendous power. It was a real festival, with all the buses, the barren land – and when Mother's voice came, live from her room in the Ashram, it was overwhelming. There definitely was a very special force present that day.

Auroville could never have started, even less have materialized to the extent it has today, if there were no Divine power sustaining it. Other memory: I would go every morning with all the information to Mother. One day she told me: so far, I have received ideas about buildings, this, that. The real Auroville, it will take 200 years. So it's obvious to me that the change of consciousness is the first requirement. We put the cart before the horse if we talk about physical transformation before having realized that.

A thousand paths

From Udar Pinto's reminiscences...

Mother involved me on three occasions regarding Auroville. The first was the inauguration of Auroville. There was a plan: two young representatives of each country would come and bring earth from their country and put it into that Urn. And at the same time the Charter would be read in some languages. Now Mother told me that the communist countries were refusing to participate because of one word in the Charter: the word 'divine'.

So she said, "I want you to see the Russian Consul-General."

I was surprised because I knew nothing about it, so I complained, "Why send me?"

"You just go! Don't think of anything clever to do, I'll just put words in your mouth."

Now I'll tell you about Mother. When she asks you to do something, she arranges the circumstances beautifully. You see, I was ordered to see the Consul-General: as a complete stranger you have to make an appointment and you have to wait. I just went straight, made no appointment, and said I was from the Sri Aurobindo Ashram and I wanted to see the Consul General. Normally you don't succeed, but they said "Yes" – very naturally. It is a kind of a miracle, but you don't see it as a miracle. That is the beauty of Mother's miracles; they happen very naturally. So the man asked me to come up at once. He greeted me at the door and said, "Oh! come, come, we are so happy about this whole scheme of Auroville, the first international city of

Udar Pinto and Auroville's Chief Architect Roger Anger.

the whole world; but the one thing stopping us is about 'the Divine' ..."

Now I didn't think of what to say and I'll tell you how Mother works. I said, "All right, Consul-General, if you can't take the word "Divine", let us see what you can take. Do you believe in progress?"

"Of course we believe in progress, communism has to progress." "Progress towards what?" "Go on progressing, progressing towards something!"

I said, "Suppose I say, progress towards perfection?"

He began to ponder, then he embraced me, "You have given a new slogan for our party. I will inform my government immediately." Then I waited for him to cool down a little bit and said, "And what about ultimate perfection?" "Now you begin to become a philosopher, ultimate doesn't mean anything."

He was a happy fellow, with a good sense of humour.

I said, "All right, you don't like it because it means nothing. And what about zero and infinity, they mean nothing and yet you have to use them in mathematics. You Russians are very good in mathematics, if you remove zero and infinity they'll shoot you!" (laughs)

"Yes", he said; he was a very sweet man. Then he said, "All right, I'll accept ultimate perfection. Then what?" I said, "That is the Divine." "What! That is the Divine?" "Look Consul-General, any effort you follow, ultimately you reach the Divine. There are a thousand paths and ultimately you reach the Divine." "Is that so? All right then," he said, "we can take that."

Udar Pinto together with Auroville's Chief Architect Roger Anger.

The day the balloon went up

It was like this, wasn't it? A long-time Aurovilian tries to remember...

One of my earliest memories as a child was being held out of the window of a railway carriage as the train wound its way along the side of a valley, revealing first one end of the train and then the other, my grandfather twisting me first one way, then the other as he sang out, "There's where we come from; there's where we go."

Forty years later I had a similar experience as I came onto Auroville land for the first time for the inaugural ceremony. The bus in which we travelled had turned the corner near Hope and suddenly people were standing up, pointing. There were no trees then,

remember, and the views were long. Some people pointed way across the barren fields to an orange meteorological balloon tethered near a distant banyan tree; some pointed behind to all the buses that followed us, while others were pointing ahead to all the buses going around the next bend. Everyone started to laugh.

We had arrived at the Ashram four months earlier. The first we heard of Auroville was when Mother told us we were to work for it. And although in the meantime we had been given work in Ashram departments we had started to involve ourselves in the preparation for the opening ceremony.

Over the years I've been trying to recall it as a glorious time when we all worked harmoniously together under the directions of the Mother. But it wasn't like that. It was a mess.

For four months everyone disagreed, argued, contradicted each other, worked at cross-purposes, fought for their own version of things. In mid-February, for example, we were still undecided how even to identify the country whose representatives were going to walk up the spiral pathway with their samples of earth to put in the Urn. The man who wanted flags, knowing that we now lacked time to get them, stormed out of one meeting in search of an Ashram artist who would agree to silkscreen 124 different flags. "Have you seen some of those flags?" someone shouted after him. Before the reverberations of the slammed door had faded away someone else came up with another idea: how about making a gigantic jigsaw puzzle of a world map, so that everyone coming up to the Urn could be able to fit his country's shape into the general picture? I got up and quit, right then and there, but I realized before I had even got out the door that no one had invited me to be a part of that committee in the first place.

On the 27th February I went to bed convinced that the next day would bring about the biggest shambles the world had ever seen.

I awoke at first light to a fantastic day, crows in the palm trees, kites in the sky, a faint shushing of small waves breaking on the shore. We left the house early, clad in white; everyone that day seemed to be wearing white. The buses were lined up in the streets between the Ashram and the sea-front. I rather think each one had a number, for I remember looking for a particular bus, suddenly filled with a keen apprehension that if I wasn't careful I might miss out on something fundamentally important. Looking back I always fancied I wore some kind of badge identifying me as something or other, although that strikes me now as unlikely. On reflection I think it must have been some symbolic tribal feeling I was experiencing, the badge perhaps a declaration of some inner commitment.

I suppose it was catching, this apprehension, for it resulted in a bit of scurrying to and fro with calling out to children and wayward aunties and old grannies. But finally everyone was on board and the buses, in convoy, moved off. Still it wasn't until we'd turned onto the dirt road that we realized how many of us there were. I'm tempted to say that there were a hundred buses but that couldn't be, could it? All I know is that it seemed that every available vehicle of every conceivable description had been put into use that day. And if it hadn't been for the fact that the road had been watered before we got there we'd have raised a cloud of dust to rival the one caused by the eruption of Krakatoa.

The road sort-of ended near the present-day Matrimandir parking lot. How could they all fit in there? You're forgetting that there were no trees, none at all, except a scraggly grove of palmyras and a young banyan giving shape to a wide open space.

We all descended and began to shuffle our way through the sand across perfectly flat ground to what looked like some raised earthworks topped by a temporary structure of casuarinas and cloth. Blue, I think, the cloth. Closer, we could see it was the lip of a circular depression in the earth, the covered shelter circling the rim. Down in the depression, off-centre, clearly significant, was the stylized lotus bud, the only thing with any look of permanence to it. Settling without speech some sat in chairs, some on mats in the shade, some out in the sun. A section had been reserved for the people from the nearby villages, and although it was a large enclosure already you could see it was going to be inadequate. You could see people coming from every direction across the fields.

Red earth, green from the tree, people in white, orange balloon against the blue sky, the billowing blue cloth giving an occasional explosive clap above us.

You know I could be making all this up. For really I don't know; I'll never be sure. It could all be merely a striving to put myself back into a place the significance of which I shall, I suppose, never be able, fully, to comprehend. I'm tempted to put down the names of people I know were present in the belief that there is safety in numbers. But I don't actually remember who I sat next to. I don't know to whom I spoke. I don't know who I met. Sometimes I wonder what part of me was present...

It was all so simple, really, so splendid.

As 10:30 approached silence fell. There was, I think, the sound of a gong. And then The Mother's voice. It was transmitted live, directly from her upstairs room in the Ashram, a fact which seemed to add immediacy to the message.

Have I given the impression, earlier, that laughter, that day, came easy? Well I'll tell you, the day had changed. What was going on now was no laughing matter. If there was a suggestion behind the words it was this: Listen to me. Listen. And listen we did as if our lives depended upon it.

The newspaper said the ceremony lasted 75 minutes. I'll accept that. After all it's their business to measure things. Certainly a lot seemed to have happened by the time it was over. I do remember Mother's flag with its golden wheel resplendent on a blue field being carried up by Kiran in the beginning just when they started the reading of the translations of the Charter into the different languages. And near the end I remember Fabienne and Kalya with the Auroville flag – it was the first time we'd seen it; we didn't even know it existed. In between I remember something of the procession of young people, some of them in their national dress, the boys with their packets of earth, the girls with the signs, beribboned in their national colours, which announced their country. I particularly remember the Russian participants for they were little children which somehow seemed most aptly to embody the spirit of the occasion.

When the last young couple had come back from the Urn Nolinida went up to seal the lotus. He seemed to be up there an awful long time. I got the feeling that Mother was supervising his masonry work. At last, I thought, she's finally got someone who will do what he's told.

When he came down I suppose we all came down. Sunil's music ended. The crowds dispersed. We wandered off to the exhibition around the banyan tree. We got fed, every single one of us. We looked up at the balloon, and around at the bleak landscape, and then we got back on the bus. (Isn't it amazing how it always takes more buses to get people home after an event than it does to get them out in the first place?) And so we went back to Pondy, not to come back, any of us, for six months.

So that's the way it was, was it? Well I wouldn't actually swear to it. After all it's a long time ago. And I've got a terrible memory. And I have this habit of what I don't remember I make up. But only in the details, I think. But surely you can tell it was something, can't you? You can feel it was something real, momentous?

You must also have realized, as we did ourselves much later, that while we were squabbling away The Mother was getting things done. Would it have been better, do you think, an even more glorious day, if we had stayed out of her way altogether? Perhaps. And perhaps not. I suppose she knew what she was doing when, in her infinite wisdom, she did something foolish, and let us participate.

Nolinida, Mother's secretary and also secretary of the Sri Aurobindo Ashram, seals the urn at the heart of the Auroville Amphitheatre.

An electric shock

On the evening of 28th February Hema Arora sent the following letter to Mother...

Douce Mère,

The inauguration ceremony of Auroville this morning was an unforgettable experience. Out of chaos and disorder everything worked towards harmony and beauty.

I had been selected to represent Iraq during the inauguration ceremony but people from that country arrived so I was shifted to represent Yugoslavia. Unluckily for me people from that country also reached Auroville at the last moment. Then I was made a Turk, but to my utter dismay people from Turkey also panted in at the last second. Finally I was given the banner of China, and that too communist China. You can very well imagine my feelings at that moment! Well, I can at least boast of being the only person to have changed her nationality four times in a single hour.

Douce Mère, as the ceremony started all the muddle and confusion were forgotten. I could feel your presence among us so powerfully, so very concretely that nothing else mattered. An ardent aspiration mounted upwards for the realisation of this beautiful dream of yours; of Auroville - city of Harmony. It was a moment when "earth grew unexpectedly divine".

It was no longer of any importance which country I represented or which countries others stood for, what counted most at that time was that we were present at this very solemn and historic hour in our march towards perfection.

Reading the Charter of Auroville

As I walked into the arena with China's flag in my hands an electric shock seemed to have passed through my being, emptying it of all thoughts and feelings and "touching the moment with eternity".

Nearly everyone present must have felt something, for there was a trance-like quality in their gait when they entered the arena.

Douce Mère, today was really a very beautiful and memorable day.

Thank you and good-night.

Theodora Karnasch reading the Auroville Charter in German (left top)
Maggi Lidchi-Grassi reading the Charter of Auroville in Spanish (left bottom)

Mother's magic

Gauri, the daughter of Udar Pinto, remembers...

My friend and I, both young teachers in SAICE, were put in charge of serving meals to the youth who were being sent from the various embassies in Delhi for the inauguration ceremony of Auroville. A young girl and boy, representing their country, had been asked to come. They were mostly teenagers who were not in the least interested in spiritual life and not at all clear about what was happening.

To keep them occupied till the inauguration, another of our teachers was given the responsibility of taking them out to see the well-known places around Pondicherry and keeping them out of mischief.

As the Coner House (the new dining hall for our students) was not yet quite ready, we had to rearrange the classrooms of our school during mealtime to feed these youngsters. The food was cooked with special care at a private house and then brought to the school. These children had a good appetite and we were kept busy. Some of them even showed up drunk or in a bad temper. Naturally we were apprehensive about the way these children would behave on the great day. I'd like to mention here that what impressed me was how dignified and courteous the ones who came from Africa were. Of course, they were older.

On the morning of the 28th of February 1968 there was great excitement. A bus load of our students who would carry the flag and the soil of the many countries that could not send their representatives also went with these foreign children. In fact, there were so many going

Poppo Pingel and Petra Erdmann, representing Germany, in the waiting crowd of delegates.

to Auroville that it was hard to find a seat. But we hopped on to a moving vehicle and eventually reached the place where the lotus bud Urn stood.

Soon the ceremony began, and it was so beautiful and moving that it will stay in my memory for ever. Mother's voice, arriving live from Pondicherry, reached us at the exact time that the first pair started ascending the ramp towards the Urn.

We of the meal group could hardly believe our eyes. We knew only too well how unruly and unkempt some of these embassy children were. But now there was a transformation. They were so neat and clean and well-behaved, walking up the ramp like disciplined angels. Mother's magic had worked in them.

The rest is well known – how beautiful and perfect that day was, so full of a very special atmosphere and presence.

An expectant hush charged the atmosphere

Ramakant Navelkar from the Sri Aurobindo Ashram remembers...

Poppo Pingel signing the scroll

I am glad to tell that I was one of the most fortunate human beings – amongst the millions of human beings who were on earth – to be present at Auroville's Inauguration Ceremony on 28 February 1968.

The atmosphere was charged with an expectant hush. It reminded us that "It was the hour before the Gods awake" – the first line of Sri Aurobindo's epic poem 'Savitri'. The Mother's recorded voice proclaimed the Charter of Auroville to the world. The Mother's reading had such a power that it stunned the minds of the people present. This was followed by the placard-bearers of many countries and all the States of India.

Each State of India and each country represented had brought earth from its soil and it was put in the Urn at the centre of the amphitheatre. Nolini Kanta Gupta – the Secretary of the Ashram – was the last, and sealed the Urn. We returned to the Ashram, our beings saturated with deep inner conviction about the spiritual destination of humanity.

"Let's make our peace now"

Poppo Pingel remembers...

Poppo first heard about Auroville in 1967. He was teaching in Osmania University, Hyderabad, and one day the German Consul, Carlos Pfauter, gave a party for all the Germans living in the area. "He said to me, 'You're an architect and some people want to build an international city near Pondicherry. They will send us an invitation to attend the inauguration. Why don't you go and represent Germany?' I said OK. I didn't expect anything would come of it: in those days so many people promised so many things, and most of them were bluff. But this one turned out to be true!"

At that time Poppo knew nothing about Mother or Sri Aurobindo. However, at Christmas there was a tradition for everybody in his organization to receive gifts. And the previous year one of his presents was a German biography of Sri Aurobindo. "I put it aside unread. In those days, I wasn't interested in reading: I felt that to read was to lose time, to lose life. However, after the invitation to the inauguration of Auroville actually arrived I told myself that as I was going on an official visit to a place named after him, I'd better read the book. When I first came across direct quotations from Sri Aurobindo I got something like shivers – it was the first touch."

A telegram from the German Embassy in Delhi told Poppo to go to the Consulate in Madras, where he would meet the other German representative at the inauguration – a nurse working in the Nilgiris – and pick up the German soil which would be placed in the Urn. Later, while waiting at the Madras bus-stand, he met Bibash, the nephew of Nirodbaran. "We talked all the way to Pondy, then he took me to Corner House where all the delegates to the inauguration were eating."

Various tours and talks were organised for the delegates over the next four days, and Poppo just allowed himself to be carried along. The day of the inauguration began with the delegates handing over their soil and getting it back in a small ceramic bowl decorated with their national colours and emblems. During the wait for the bus, Poppo was queueing with the two young French delegates. "We were laughing and joking together. I saw these blue flowers and I plucked one and gave them to the French saying, 'Our countries have been at war for centuries. Let's make our peace now.' They immediately agreed. So I put the flower I'd plucked into the French bowl of earth and they put a flower into ours. And those flowers of unity went into the Urn with our countries' earth."

When the buses turned onto the Auroville plateau, Poppo's heart sank. "All I saw was barren sandy soil. It reminded me of Bihar and I was convinced that working here was impossible. At the same time I was fascinated by the idea of human unity and I liked being engulfed in the internationalism of the thing. That was something I'd been looking for all my life."

There was no rehearsal for the ceremony itself. "People in white were running round organizing us into the correct sequence, giving us instructions. Most attendees were sitting in the shade of the shamianas erected around the amphitheatre, but the delegates had to wait in the sun. And it was hot! Everything went very slowly. When it was our turn to go up to the Urn the girl carried the placard and I carried the bowl of soil. I poured it in, and then I bent over and peered inside. I saw a pile of dry sand. At that moment, I heard a muffled giggle go round the amphitheatre. Obviously they were laughing at my curiosity. Afterwards we were guided to a table where we had to put our signature and write our country's name on a large silk scroll. When I wrote my hand was shaking: it was like being at the inauguration of something huge, like the Olympic Games."

There was an exhibition under the Banyan Tree, but after the ceremony all that Poppo and the other delegates wanted was something to drink. "But all the drinks were finished. So when we returned to Pondy we went and had some beers with our French friends."

A few days later Poppo wrote to his parents: "I feel strongly that this will be the town of my life because it cannot be otherwise, Auroville, the town of the future. What I experienced here is proof that the direction of my thinking has found a brother ... "

Back in Hyderabad he talked to everybody he knew about Auroville. "I still didn't think I could actually ever work there but, like a cosmic law, something was coming slowly down. A few years later I was back. For good."

All the villages were present

Damodaran Harikrishnan remembers...

Damodaran Harikrishnan from the village of Kuilapalayam is one of the earliest Tamil men who helped to bridge the gap between Aurovilians and the locals. Now he is almost 60 years old. Some of his sons and daughters are Aurovilians active in the community. February 28th 1968 is a day that stands out in his memory.

"There was a festive atmosphere that day. There was a huge crowd and people came in buses from Pondicherry. The entire village of Kuilapalayam was there. Not just from Kuilapalayarn, but people from all surrounding villages – Edayanchavadi, Kottakarai. People were from all parts of India and from over 120 countries. They brought earth from their lands; it was mingled together in the Urn. This was to be a universal city (sarvadesa nagaram) meant for all human beings. It was Mother's vision, and what a noble concept it was! To work together in unity, in honesty, and selflessly for all. Now it feels different. I feel people should not be selfish looking for their own gain and just start businesses. Auroville has to be different from the rest of the world. I feel Mother's dreams for this land have to be remembered and the people here have to recommit themselves to its ideals. Only then will this day continue to have meaning and this land can be the universal city it is meant to be."

Villagers visiting the Auroville exhibition near the Banyan tree

The grandest day of my life

Tapas Bhatt remembers the preparations...

My memories of Auroville go back to the years 1965 or 1966. I was a pupil of the Sri Aurobindo International School in the Ashram. In those years Roger Anger used to visit the Mother to talk about Auroville. Afterwards he would sometimes come to our class and give us big sheets and colour pencils, and ask us to make a drawing of how we imagined the ideal city. That play of my imagination was my first contact with Auroville. I must have been 14 at the time. The stories of Mother's ideal city filled us children with incredible enthusiasm.

Late 1967, beginning of 1968, many ashramites joined forces to build the first roads in Auroville. We went by bus, and sweated it out to make the road from Kuilapalayam to the amphitheatre. One night in Pondicherry I dreamt of that landscape of red earth, yellow sun and blue sky, where I was all alone in silence. Somehow, it was an initiation into Auroville.

From February 21st to late in the night of 27th the grounds around the Urn and the Banyan tree were prepared. Buses took us every day early morning and we would return late evening. My job was to decorate with kolams the bottom of a big pond, a job that was done together with some village women and Roger Anger. Once the paint had dried, water was put into the pond.

When I came home on the 27th, very tired and covered with red earth, my father told me that Tanmaya, a teacher from the school, had left a message that the next day I was going to participate in the ceremony, representing Syria.

February 28th. We left at 5 a.m. There was a fleet of more than 50 buses waiting for all the delegates and us children near the Ganesh temple in Pondicherry. We boarded, and then started what is probably the grandest day of my life. The buses went to Jipmer hospital, from there passing Auro-Orchard and Hope to Edayanchavadi and then to the amphitheatre. Right from Jipmer, through Edayanchavadi village all the way up to the Urn, crowds were cheering on both sides of the road. When we arrived, we were seated under the canopies set up all around the amphitheatre.

Pathways were planned out, and then a boy and a girl representing each country would walk up the pathway to the Urn, carrying a placard with the name of that country, and deposit the earth of the country into the Urn, while the Charter was read out in that country's language. If there was no earth available, we put salt. Mother had selected Ashram children to represent those countries from which there were no official representatives. There was a very powerful atmosphere, especially when we heard the direct broadcast of Mother reading her message from her room in the Ashram. The entire amphitheatre, full of people, fell silent. There was the red earth, the hot sun, the blue sky, and the buses, and people were like little ants in a new cosmos. It was a surrealistic image with a very special atmosphere: a joining of a strong human aspiration that Auroville is going to be a grand dream to work for. And there was an incredible feeling of togetherness – people from all different parts of the world joining in that aspiration.

When we had done our bit, there was a big exhibition around the Banyan tree. There were big blocks of circular concrete for sitting, and everybody was having a good time. Photos were taken, and then somebody discovered an image of The Mother in the Banyan tree. While she was reading her Message from her room in the Ashram, she was also present at Auroville.

Then we went back by bus to Pondicherry. There was a big function in the garden of the office of the Sri Aurobindo Society. There was a question and answer session with all the delegates, a lively interaction, which kept us together for a day or two longer.

That ceremony had changed something in me. In the months and years that followed, I kept coming to Auroville, by bus or cycle, for doing some digging or some other work. I wouldn't lose a single opportunity to come. My classmates were equally enthusiastic. For us it was a sense of picnic. Between 1968 and 1977, when I finally moved here, we would often come on Saturdays, doing night duty at the Matrimandir.

Memories of the Inauguration and lead-up to it

Kiran Poddar remembers...

Kiran Poddar's memories, recorded below from an interview with her, are of special interest because of her family connection to Sri Navajata, her personal contact with the Mother, and the special role that Mother asked her to play in the actual inauguration (see below).

Planning, preparation, and Mother's directive

Planning of Auroville's inauguration started in 1967. At that time Kiran (then aged 19) was a student at SAICE. Their family house was the hub, the centre of planning and coordination for everything related to the inauguration. However, it was only after Kiran completed her studies on October 31st that she became involved herself, when Mother told her quite specifically that she wanted her "to work for Auroville; to help your father [Sri Navajata] with Auroville work." This work then became quite naturally like an extension of her life in the Ashram.

People like Roger Anger, and Gilbert Gauché, a PR man from France who had experience of planning major events elsewhere in the world, were coming to Navajata (henceforth 'Nava') with their ideas and requests for the inauguration, such as to have a big balloon flying high above the banyan tree on the day.

Indira Gandhi, Prime Minister of India, together with Navajata, Chief Executive, Sri Aurobindo Society and Auroville and Roger Anger, Chief Architect of Auroville, 6 October 1969.

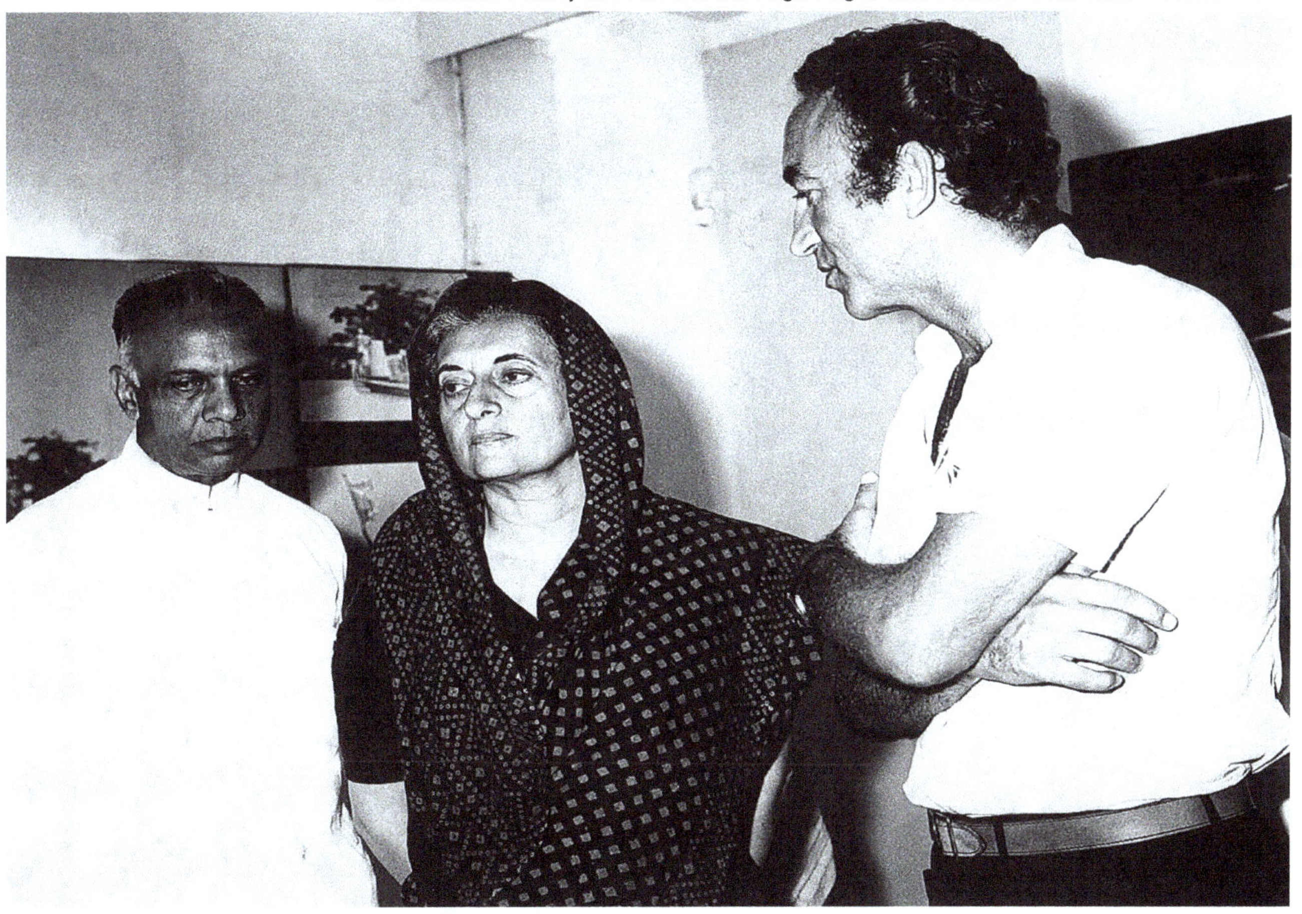

Meanwhile, as usual, everything was automatically being shared with and conveyed to Mother, who was interested in all the details of plans for the day, and was keen to know where matters stood on everything.

Acquiring the land for the inauguration

As at late 1967, not all the land needed for the inauguration had been acquired. Every day Nava was reporting on the situation (and other such matters) to the Mother, because she had placed special emphasis on the importance of getting the land, saying strongly and clearly, "I want it (the land) to be bought…" All Nava could do was reassure her that it would be bought – if her grace was there!

Meanwhile, the pressure to buy the land in time was leading to sometimes difficult negotiations with the village owners by the various individuals working with Nava on this crucial matter, because the owners were already aware that something big was being planned for the plateau site, and naturally saw an opportunity to make some good money in the process.

Independent of the negotiations, Nava conveyed to all the village headmen that they and their people were invited to and also expected to attend the inaugural event.

As an example of the contagious atmosphere surrounding preparations for the inauguration, it was around this time that a young Englishman named Don Fisher arrived for the first time in Pondy with his Land-Rover, and – despite knowing nothing about the Auroville project and its inauguration beforehand, and having no previous connection with the Ashram – immediately offered to make his vehicle available, with himself as

Centre, wearing glasses, Dr. Salah-El-Din Tewfik, UNESCO's Chief of Mission, New Delhi

driver, to help in any way he could. He often ran Nava out to the inauguration site, to meet village headmen, etc, all at his own expense.

Transport

One of the Ashram departments inevitably involved in preparations for the event was the Transport Dept, which had to work out how best to make use of the department's vehicles for the occasion. Other transport details such as the logistics of the route from Pondy to the Auroville site; who would go at what time with what vehicle(s); and the pick-up points, etc, to get Ashram and other people from Pondy to the site, were mainly taken care of by young Ashram volunteers, who were being coordinated by Mona Sarkar of SAICE (the Sri Aurobindo International Centre for Education).

However, more vehicles were needed than the Ashram had available, specially buses, so Nava used a personal contact – an industrialist friend who was a devotee of Mother, and who ran with Mother's blessings an organization called "Progress Transport" – to arrange for a large fleet of buses to be available on the day. There were at least 20-30 of them, maybe as many as 50, that eventually formed a huge convoy from Pondy to the site, together with many private cars, the owners of which had also offered to help with transport.

Pondicherry State co-operatrion

Pondy State government was fully supportive of the whole event. The Police closed off all side roads from Pondy to the site to ensure smooth flow of the many buses, VIP cars and other vehicles taking everyone to the site.

Exhibition under the Banyan tree

The The Ashram recording section was handling the live relay of Mother's voice from her room in Pondicherry to the inauguration site in Auroville. The relay was not through the city's main telephone exchange but through the Pondicherry All India Radio telephone line and they had blocked all other lines so that there would not be any interface or disturbance.

These and other gestures showed how widespread and deeply felt was the support for the event within Pondicherry's administration. The feelings in regard to the importance of the event went far beyond just the Ashram, and also embraced the town of Pondicherry.

The Ashram and the inauguration

The inauguration was a big, BIG event in the life of the Ashram at that time. In fact one can say that the whole Ashram became involved in one way or another following its announcement. The actual programme for the event, with transport details, timings, etc, was announced by way of a beautiful hand-painted poster – signed and "Blessed" by Mother – during the week leading up to 28th February.

In announcing the event, mention was made of the plan to bring two young people representing every nation and state of India for the day, and the need to take care of them by way of providing accommodation and generally looking after them. It was stated that it would be preferable for the accommodation to be in Ashram buildings and with Ashram families, and not to have them stay in local hotels, of which – anyway – there were not so many in those days. SAICE took up this responsibility, and via its teachers and students found the needed beds and rooms for all the expected attendees. In fact they took full responsibility for looking after them, making them feel welcome, and showing them around. This was specially important, as some were expected well ahead of the 28th and therefore needed this sort of help and hospitality in the lead-up to the actual day.

As the day of the inauguration drew closer, everyone in the Ashram became increasingly focused on it, and began to work together in a wonderful spirit of mutual harmony and goodwill. They set aside whatever personal problems they might have been dealing with at the time,

and made the coming inauguration the number one priority, the focus of their lives at that moment, seeing it as something of great importance to Mother's work. It was something that had to happen – the first beginnings of making Mother's 'Dream' a reality.

Ashram students representing absent countries

The French teacher in the Education Department (Monsieur Raymond, renamed Tanmaya by Mother) was the coordinator who chose the Ashram students to stand in for unrepresented countries and perform other associated roles. This 'standing-in' for representatives became necessary because, although some countries sent both a boy and a girl as requested (usually connected with their Embassy in Delhi), some sent only one, and some sent none.

Mother's involvement and presence

As far back as the autumn of 1967, Mother had chosen Kiran and her brother Vijay to be the first to go to the Urn, carrying soil from the Samadhi with the Auroville Charter, the latter handwritten by Mother and contained in a sealed stainless steel cylinder.

On learning about this, Kiran tried to persuade Mother to be physically present at the event herself, but she replied that that was not possible. However, she implied that SHE WOULD BE THERE, making this assurance when she told Kiran and Vijay to come to her room early at 8.00 a.m. on the morning of the 28th, with the words… "You will come here to my room on the morning of the inauguration, and then (touching her heart) take me with you to the inauguration" that is on a subtle plane.

On arrival at her room on the actual morning, they found quite a number of others also there connected with the event. Mother then gave Kiran and Vijay the ceramic bowl (which Kiran still has) containing the Samadhi soil, handing it to her as though she was handing over the most precious and valuable thing on the planet, together with the hand-written Charter (Mother had done two; what happened to the other one nobody knows) which was then placed in a stainless steel cylinder (approx 60-70 cms long), presumably made by Harpagon Workshop. She then wanted to know exactly how they would place the cylinder in the Urn. Others present gave their ideas, one of which was to tie a sky-blue ribbon around the cylinder to lower it vertically into the Urn. Mother agreed to this, and then asked about the flag: "How are you going to hold it?" Then Mother spontaneously took the flag in her own hands, and – with great strength and force – proceeded to show Kiran exactly how it was to be held. (For Mother, every single detail was important – even how to place the Charter cylinder and the soil sample into the Urn.)

The soil of each nation

An important detail to be organized was arranging the soil to be put in the Urn by representatives of each nation. It was simply asked of each nation that they should bring "some soil" from their country, but quite a number of national representatives brought special soil from places sacred or precious to that country (in the same way that when an Indian temple is to be built, water from the 7 holy rivers of India is brought to the site).

Feeding the thousands of attendees

Following agreement to provide a rice-based lunch packet for everyone attending at the site after the actual inaugural event, Dyuman – who was at that time in charge of the Ashram Dining Hall – took full responsibility, and undertook the arrangements to provide at least 10,000 such lunches, maybe 15,000, on the assumption that some 5,000 would be needed for the Ashram/Pondy people and perhaps another 10,000 for the many villagers

Excavation work for the Amphitheatre.

expected to attend. The idea was that the lunch packet could be opened and eaten at the inauguration site without need for formal seating arrangements.

This was a huge challenge, because the Dining Hall people had never done anything comparable before, specially to feed so many people so far away (transport alone was one of the logistic problems, plus handing out the food packets in an orderly manner), but it went very well, to the satisfaction of everyone attending. Water was of course also laid on, from a well approx 1 km from the site.

Preparing the site

There were no roads on the plateau at that time, so the Ashram boys were going out in the evening and working at night for several weeks before the event to create the road from today's Certitude corner to the Banyan tree.

So many details had to be worked out. Meanwhile Nata was collaborating with Roger A. on the actual construction of the Amphitheatre and other features of the site (the Ashram Garden Section, for example, was working to provide lots of lotus flowers and potted plants for the day). Keet roofing was used around the rim of the Amphitheatre for shading from the sun, specially where chairs were set out for people like the VIPs (such as Mr. Tewfiq, Head of the UNESCO office in Delhi), though on the day many people just sat or stood on the earth slopes of the Amphitheatre in the full sun.

The Urn

The reinforced concrete Urn, designed by Roger, was cast at Coco Garden under the directions of Harpagon

Workshop (run by Udar). On completion it was marble-chip covered by (Sicilian-born) French Aurovilian Vincenzo Maiolini.

Exhibition at banyan tree
Regarding the exhibition that was to be set up close to the banyan tree, Roger had arranged for circular platforms to be built on which exhibition panels were mounted with Mother's messages on Auroville, its purpose and aims, the Charter, etc. There were lots of lotuses and other flowers around.

The balloon
Following Gilbert Gauché's suggestion of a hydrogen balloon over the banyan tree on the day, Nava had used his contacts to get hold of one, but it didn't materialize with the hydrogen gas and specialist engineer until the day before i.e. February 27th. It was then immediately taken up to the site, and worked on overnight to have it ready the next morning. Sure enough, on the morning of the 28th it could be seen flying high in the sky above the banyan tree from as far away as Promesse.

Crowd control and coordination of the programme
Student volunteers from the Ashram Physical Education Department, coordinated by Mona Sarkar, took responsibility for looking after the various sections of the crowd, guiding the VIPs, delegates, youth representatives, Ashramites, local village people, etc (the latter were mostly taken direct care of by the Ashram/Society people who had been involved in land negotiations with them).

Banyan tree and later nearby keet hut

Udar was the key person acting as Master of Ceremonies during the event, though Nolini was also there (he sealed the Urn once it was full with all the earth samples), and likewise Nava and all the other high-profile Ashramites.

Sequence of the event

Mother had set the time of the inauguration as 10.30am.

First item on the programme was Mother reading, from her room in the Ashram, the text "Greetings to all men of goodwill. Are invited to Auroville…" (Kiran found it very moving that Mother was issuing this invitation to the whole world at that moment.) followed by the Charter of Auroville in French.

Kiran and Vijay, representing the Ashram and also carrying the scroll of the Charter of Auroville in Mother's handwriting, then started the sequence of young people carrying the name placard and soil of their state or country (the states first) in alphabetical order, while at the same time the Charter was being read out in many languages, 16 in total, each reading whenever possible coinciding with the youngsters from that country going to the Urn (the English reading was by Norman Dowsett; the Tamil by Amritada, who had been responsible for its translation into that language; the Sanskrit by Madhav Pandit; the German by Eckhardt's wife Theodora Karnasch). Last of all came Kalya and Fabienne with the flag of Auroville and the earth of Auroville. Nolini then stepped forward to seal the Urn.

Impressions and reactions – personal and general

When Kiran had been in Mother's room just before leaving for the inauguration, she had had an overwhelming feeling of something immense and powerful being brought down by Mother for humanity at the time. She felt that Mother was pouring her force into all involved, into Nava, Roger, Nata and others, as well as into herself and Vijay and everyone else in the room and beyond. This feeling stayed with Kiran throughout the event, to the point that she didn't feel it was any longer just her normal limited self that was there at the event,

but that a part of Mother was also there with her, and with everyone else up on the plateau. She felt that Mother's whole vision and force for the realisation of Auroville had been implanted in all those who had been present in her room, and that they were now all part of a historically important moment during which Mother was bringing down something of great importance to the whole world i.e. to Planet Earth and everyone on it. Commenting on the actual inaugural event, she said: "It all went so smoothly; it was as though Mother herself was directly overseeing and conducting everything. Everyone was so enthusiastic to be playing a part and involved in something so huge, to be actually participating in such an important event. I had the impression that this feeling was shared by everyone, by all the 10,000 to 15,000 people on the plateau at the time. It was as though Mother was bringing down something great and immense, truly giving something to the whole world, to all humanity – an opportunity."

No doubt many others also felt something similar, because Kiran says that some of the letters written by the young participants and students after the inauguration were very moving and beautiful.

Press coverage and Mother's image in the banyan

The day after the inauguration the Indian Express newspaper had a big write-up on the event, covering the whole front page, with a large photo of Nolini sealing the Urn. It may have been in this photo that Mother's image appeared in the banyan tree, as seen from the opposite side of the Amphitheatre (with the Urn in line with the tree). Looking at the photo, people felt they could see Mother's head outlined just above the Urn in the tree, formed by the shaping of the leaves and branches with the sky behind. Many people remarked on this as being an indication of "Mother's presence".

Later, after the event, when Kiran next saw Mother, Mother remarked, "I believe the whole event went beautifully. You saw that photo in the paper? Some people say that they could see an image of me in the tree." It was at this point that Kiran remembered Mother telling her and Vijay to come to her room on the morning of the 28th and saying – tapping her chest in the area of the heart – "take me with you, here, to the inauguration. Those people who are sincere will feel me there."

Kiran had the feeling that when Mother remarked on the apparent image of herself in the photo, she was quietly reminding Kiran of what she had said, and confirming that she had, in fact, been present at the event.

Mother and the banyan

It seems that Mother had a close association with the Banyan tree, because in the early stages of preparing the inauguration site the spirit of the tree communicated to her that it was disturbed by all that was going on around it, and was not happy with how it was being treated. Following this subtle communication, Mother called Nata, who was coordinating work at the site, and asked him to investigate what was happening to the tree. This led to discovery that carpenters had hammered nails into the tree while preparing a work bench around it. Mother sent a special message via Nata to ensure that this sort of disrespectful behaviour towards the tree was immediately stopped.

After the inauguration, again the spirit of the tree came to Mother, this time to tell her how lonely it felt after all the activity around it over the past 2-3 months. Mother's response was to encourage the start of the first settlements in Auroville. This was made easier by the fact that Mother had already indicated at the time when land was being bought where a first borewell should be dug, by using a 'needle' over a map to pinpoint its position. It had proved to be an excellent source of good water.

Exhibition under the Banyan tree

Parts of the exhibition under the Banyan tree designed by Paolo Tommasi

Plan for the above exhibition

It was a magic moment!

Paolo Tommasi remembers...

"Who was the Mother? Who could understand what she was doing? Everything she gave came from such a high level; she was so kind. She was a genius in architecture. She looked human, but there was something else, something that came from a different level, beyond the mind. Her magnetism was so strong. I had the opportunity to be with her many times.

"I worked with Nathan and Roger. I still have the letter in which she asked me to collaborate with her in this great work. I was very young at that time, and I walked sometimes to Auroville by foot. There were no roads; I would come back covered with red dust, red from head to foot.

"Mother asked me to prepare an exhibition for the inauguration site, and I proposed to her to do this around the banyan tree. She agreed to this, but warned me: 'Please do not hammer any nails into the tree. I am in contact with the tree and I can feel it!'

"With the help of a team of volunteers we put up photo panels with quotes from Sri Aurobindo and the Mother, and also drawings from Champaklal. I collected

all the material that I could find on the aim and purpose of Auroville.

"Then Mother asked me to carry on the inauguration day the banner of Italy, but I don't like to be in a big crowd of people. I didn't want to go there, and so I asked Mother, "Can I please, instead, stay with you here? I can stay outside on the staircase." And she agreed to this.

"So I was sitting outside her room on the day, at the moment when she read out the Charter of Auroville and her voice was recorded live by All India Radio and broadcast by loudspeakers to the Amphitheatre, where thousands of people were waiting for the start of the ceremony.

"Mother's evolutionary work is very mysterious; we don't understand her ways. It is a way to awaken our consciousness out of the unconscious. On another level, everything is already here. We just have to try to understand. What is important is never to lose our trust."

Bruno Petris resting at the exhibition display under the Banyan tree.

It was as if a meteor from another plane crashed into the deserted land

Frederick Buxloh remembers...

"It was as if a meteor from another plane crashed into the deserted land.

"On the morning of 28th February 1968, first we could hear the noise and see the dust cloud of vehicles approaching from Pondicherry. Then came the lorries, packed full with visiting people, the buses, Ambassador cars, bullock carts, bicycles, and people walking on foot from the nearby villages. There were no good roads, just earth tracks and pathways created to reach the inauguration venue.

"At that time, my partner Shyama and I plus her three children and Auroson were already living in a hut in Auroville, on a site later named Certitude, though we also still had a flat in Pondicherry. We were not living in Auromodele, since we found the house proposed there too impractical for us with all the children. Later Piero built the concrete house which was named 'Auroson's Home'.

"I remember at that time I was helping in the organization of all the young people who were coming to represent countries from around the world; also from all over India as representatives of their states. Kireet Joshi was coordinating all this.

"Also staying in our house in Pondicherry was Vincenzo, who was building and sculpting in Coco Garden, the Ashram workshop, the Urn for the Amphitheatre to contain all the earth from the different

Part of the car parking facilities, with Ambassadors, Mercedes and other vehicles.

countries. It was not an easy task, working by hand with all the little white marble mosaic pieces to be fixed in place.

"We also started, with the help of young students from the Ashram school, to work at night to plant trees. We planted, on Mother's birthday, 21 Transformation trees. Otherwise there were no trees in sight, only the Banyan tree.

"Pranab was also part of the organisation, directing all the captains and many youngsters from the Ashram school who helped in the overall organization and preparation of the event.

"When it came to the actual inaugural function, it was Shyama who read the Auroville Charter in Swedish. Theodora Karnasch read it in German. There was also Medhananda, Yvonne Artaud, Nathan, Maggie, Gerard from Orchard. Not so many are still here with us who participated in the Inauguration.

"It was somehow a world event, with representatives from UNESCO included (there was later a meeting with them in the Ashram Library).

"Everybody had the impression that we were now going to build the city, and it would be there in 15 years time. Everyone from Pondy came and helped, believing that they were starting to build the coming City of Dawn."

Hundreds of cycles, belonging to people attending the inauguration.

I know you are on holiday but I need your help

From an interview with Gerard Cruz...

Gerard was working in a place called Mountain Paradise, an apple orchard in north India, but was visiting Pondy for Christmas, New Year and Mother's birthday annually. His connection with Roger was from 1966, when Roger was involved in constant discussion of Auroville with Mother.

Gerard had come for his annual such visit. When Mother heard he was in Pondy she asked him to come and see her, and then told him: "I know you are on holiday but I need your help." Roger had proposed him to help with renovation and extension of the Promesse premises to prepare it as a maternity centre for Auroville. This was going on, when at short notice the need had suddenly arisen for the Auroville inauguration site to be prepared. Nata, who Gerard was working closely with on Promesse, volunteered to do the work. (Nata was born in Italy. He was a very competent and good organizer, able to handle workers despite things like their demand for payment every day, etc. He had been chief engineer for the building of a city in Guatemala.) The problem was the shortage of time, because all this blew up with only around 2-3 weeks to go to the inauguration.

Nata hastily organized 3 teams of 250 local labourers, who worked in 3 shifts non-stop day and night for maybe 7-10 days to dig the Amphitheatre by hand and prepare the site according to Roger's design.

At the same time work was also in progress by Paolo Tommasi on preparing the exhibition around the banyan tree. This was a big Ashram effort, with people coming & going, and even working sometimes at night to get it ready. It was only at the last moment that the final touches were completed. Meanwhile, the work sparked an interesting incident, because early in the work Mother one night received a "complaint" from the banyan tree that it was being "mistreated". Early the next morning she informed Amrita, who called Nata, who asked Gerard to go and see what was going on.

He found that the carpenters had cut or nailed into the tree to fix their work bench against it, where they were planing the wood for the exhibition. This was immediately removed, and no further nailing or other such physical abuse was allowed.

Specific questions put to Gerard:

Q. How about the metal ring around the banyan tree?

A. It was made at Harpagon, but originally without the Tamil text that had been planned to go alongside the French and English.

Q. Who read the Charter?

A. First was Mother reading in French, and then Nolini in English.

Q. Did Nava or Roger play any role in the event?

A. No. Both were present, but that's all.

Q. What were for you the highlights of the event?

A. The fact that Mother's Dream was actually in process of being realized on the material plane. Many people sensed the scale of what was happening, because nothing comparable had ever happened previously involving the Ashram.

Q. What was the most moving aspect of the event?

A. The coming of all those young people to the Urn with their earth samples; it was very symbolic of Mother's Dream of human unity.

Q. Did you feel anything special about the event?

A. Yes, that something was actually moving in the material world to make Mother's dream a reality.

The role of Vincenzo, fabricator of the Urn

The whole inauguration concept was started by a man named Gilbert Gauché, one of Roger's many collaborators. He had a PR background in France, where he had experience of organizing big international-type events. Of course it was Mother who came up with the original idea of the inauguration, but it was GG who came up with the detailed suggestions for the actual inauguration.

A key part of his plan was to have a young couple (boy & girl) from every country contribute a small portion of their national soil into the Urn. It all happened quite quickly; everything went fast, including construction of the Urn.

The design of the Urn was done by Roger, and Mother appointed Vincenzo Maiolini to make the actual Urn in the Ashram's Harpagon workshop, even though he had done nothing like it before. Actually, Roger's design caused a big controversy, because Mother had originally done a drawing of a lotus bud for the Urn that closely resembled the one in nature, and when everyone saw Roger's design some were very unhappy with how it differed from Mother's original. (A second controversy, reported by Clare Fanning, wife of Vincenzo, arose because while Vincenzo was working he was smoking and drinking coffee, and this led to complaints by the Ashram's more austere sadhaks, who wrote to Mother: "Mother, Vincenzo is smoking in the Ashram....Mother, Vincenzo is drinking coffee in the Ashram…", to which Mother replied, "Leave Vincenzo alone.")

Ashram students drawing a Kolam

Power of effort
(Effort of Auroville)

Effort well-directed overcomes all obstacles.

Ideal of the new creation
(Ideal of Auroville)

The ideal should be progressive so that it can be realised in the future.

Sweetness of power surrendered to the Divine
(Sweetness of Auroville)

Sweetness itself becomes powerful when it is at the service of the Divine.

Charm of the new creation
(Charm of Auroville)

The new creation is attractive to all those who want to progress.

Vincenzo had to work long, long hours in Pondy over a period of 2 weeks to create the Urn structure in reinforced concrete, and then cut some 2,000 small pieces of marble to size, and fix them on the shell. He was still working on the finishing touches up to the night before the event, and it was Udar's daughter who arranged for the finished Urn to be brought up and installed in time for the actual ceremony the following day. The whole marathon effort so exhausted Vincenzo that he overslept on the morning of the inauguration, and so missed most of the actual event himself.

The Amphitheatre site had been rapidly shaped just out of red earth by directed local village workers, because there were no bulldozers or JCBs available in those days. None of the finished Amphitheatre structure that we see today was there then. In fact there was absolutely no-one and no features on the plateau at that time, not even dirt roads: no trees, no shade for miles around. It really was just a wide open space of village fields, with only the banyan on site. (The "amma" of the banyan tree was not there then; she came and took up residence in a small hut by the tree sometime later.)

When people first went out to locate the site for the inauguration i.e. the "centre" of the future township, as planned, they decided that the banyan must be what Mother had in mind, and took confirmation from a cloud formation above them that day that resembled the galaxy plan, with its centre above the tree.

The whole thing came together very well when one considers the remote circumstances in which everything had to be prepared.

Construction of the Mount at the centre of the Amphitheatre

When the actual day came it was a huge effort.

Kalya (Michel) Lemaire,
Mother's great grandson, remembers...

"I got involved because I was at the Ashram school at the time (aged 17), and when the young people of many nations started arriving from around two weeks prior to the event, mostly from Delhi, I was one of the people assigned to look after them. It was a huge logistic problem to try and bring together up to 125 pairs of kids from all over the world. I mean, how does one get them? Gilbert had gone to Delhi to arrange as many as possible through a couple of "international schools", one an American school, attended by the sons and daughters of diplomats based in embassies or consulates there. It was arranged for Indian Airlines to fly them to Madras either free or at least at a special rate. But there were not so many flights then, and typically the airline could only bring around 12 a day, so they were arriving intermittently in small numbers over the two weeks prior to the event. Others were flown in to India by their national airline e.g. Air France flew in the French kids. However, as the day of the inauguration approached it became clear that not all the countries would be represented by their own nationals, and so Ashram youngsters were selected to represent those missing. Finally it all came together; it was pretty impressive. And of course there were also two kids from each of the Indian states.

"A simultaneous problem was to get the soil of each country, because of course no-one was sitting in Delhi with a bag of their homeland soil! Many samples were flown in together with the kids, but there were so many missing that Mother was asked what do about the missing soils? She came up with the idea of using sea salt, which I thought was pretty smart, that being a substance by origin that touches the shore of practically every nation on Earth, only barring a few landlocked countries. As to how much soil, some samples were literally a pinch, others a small handful at most.

"As all these kids were coming in one by one over a period of two weeks we had to do something to keep them occupied, so we used the Ashram bus to take them on picnics, to see places like Gingee, Mahabalipuram, etc. It was a fun time for me, because I was also accompanying them and getting to know them; most were very nice kids. Sadly, I never kept in touch afterwards, because there was no e-mail in those days and regular communication would have been such an effort.

"Overall, everything was well organized. There were also cultural programmes for the young people, and Ashramites like Nava gave talks to the kids practically every day. Not on things like Sri Aurobindo's philosophy specifically, but on topics that made them aware of questions about life that could be asked, like – for example – what is the purpose of life? He did it well considering the breadth of the audience he was addressing.

"When the actual day came it was a huge effort. I can't recall the exact numbers but I have 7,000 people in mind (*5,000 is the official number usually quoted, but it could easily have been much more*). The Amphitheatre site was totally surrounded by the huge crowd, many of whom had come from the surrounding villages. And of course everyone from the Ashram was there, particularly those involved directly in the Auroville project at that time. There was a temporary seating arrangement of folding chairs under awnings for shade, specially on the eastern side where the VIPs were seated, though a considerable number of people were in the full sun.

"The Auroville Charter was read in many languages, starting with the Mother reading it first in French from her room in the Ashram via a temporary telephone line connecting her room to the speaker system on site. That was impressive.

"Regarding other languages, there had been an effort to find as many people as possible able to read the Charter in their own language, and of course to have the Charter correctly translated into that language. It was read in English by Norman Dowsett (evoking a comment by the English boy who had come to represent the UK, to the effect that Norman, although a born Englishman himself, after living in India for so long no longer spoke with a "true English-English" accent, and had spoken with an 'Indlish' type accent). As this was going on, the soil and flag bearers were coming forward one by one to the Urn to place their earth sample inside, starting with Nava's kids Vijay and Kiran, representing the Ashram, carrying earth from the Samadhi. As I recall it the boys carried the earth and the girls the flag of the country, all in alphabetical order. After placing the earth in the Urn and descending via the counter-spiral on the far side, they then assembled together in a large crowd at a point in the Amphitheatre, creating a colourful mass of the world's flags together.

"There were a few countries where they had been unable to get a boy and a girl, so sometimes there were two boys. I remember the Czechoslovakian pair being one of them, and one wearing a lungi, which made him look more like a girl – to the good-natured teasing of some people there. It was all very good natured; people were getting along well and there was a nice atmosphere throughout.

"One of the things that the Mother had specifically asked about was which, if any, countries had a problem over the event, as she felt it would be a sign of something relating to the future of that country. The Americans and Russians showed no such signs, but one of the kids that absented himself just before the event was a young man from Lebanon whose wife was expecting their baby that day; he couldn't cope with the overlap, and left. People shrugged their shoulders and thought it insignificant, but

Fabienne is holding the Auroville flag while
Kalya places the earth in the Urn

Fabienne and Kalya carrying lotus flowers
after depositing the earth in the Urn

Blossoming of the new creation
(Blossoming of Auroville)
The more we concentrate on the goal,
the more it blossoms forth and becomes precise.

Progress of the new creation
(Progress of Auroville)
Each must find the activity
favourable to his progress.

Usefulness of the new creation
(Usefulness of Auroville)
A creation which aims at teaching men
to surpass themselves.

Manifold power of the new creation
(Manifold power of Auroville)
The new creation will be
rich in possibilities.

then – as we know – Lebanon suffered subsequent terrible division and disorder for years."

Kalya went forward representing Auroville at the end of the ceremony, with his cousin Fabienne (see next text), who had been flown in specially from France. This proved to be an interesting bit of coincidental timing for her, because otherwise she would have very likely been caught up in the student riots-cum-revolution that rocked Paris in 1968. Mother commented on this, to the effect that it had been a "good thing" for her not to have been there.

On the way back from placing the earth in the Urn the participants were stopping to sign a huge scroll of paper, but Roger was afterwards unhappy with the fact that the signatures had been written haphazardly all over the place and not in a well-ordered sequence that could

have made the scroll an object for later display. It is now in the Auroville Archives.

Was there a police presence? Yes, but nothing exceptional. The police on site were from Tamil Nadu state. There were also police at points along the route from Pondy to the site to ensure smooth passage of the many vehicles, specially those carrying VIPs.

Kalya didn't meet any VIPs himself. As he put it, being just 17 at the time he wasn't particularly interested in such people at that point in his life.

Asked what was his overall feeling about the day….. "It was very impressive, very well organized. We felt we were really announcing something BIG, though immediately after the ceremony it felt like quite a come-down. So much had been planned and had happened, but now… what?"

A happiness that came from the deep feeling that somehow we were in the right place at the right time

Fabienne Bernard (Kalya's cousin) remembers.

"I must say, the most important memory for me is that we were all tremendously, intensely and quietly happy, and that happiness came from the deep feeling that somehow we were in the right place at the right time with the right persons, participating in a formidable and wonderful event that certainly would help bring more joy, beauty and friendliness to the world.

"Now that might seem a little "superlative", but that is because it was superlative. We were blessed with superlative happiness ... it was as if Her dynamic and joyful Presence was everywhere, covering the whole event, in all its details, like an "atmosphere" enveloping the whole Ashram, the whole town of Pondy and the whole area of Auroville. There was a tremendous enthusiasm, dynamism and joy ... a joy of just being there.

"I had met Mother for the first time in 1966, after travelling from Paris through the Middle-East and visiting India (Delhi, Varanasi, Agra, Fathepur-Sikri) with Roger, who was bringing on that trip his first team of architects for their first acquaintance with the concept of Auroville. We all went to Mother together, and one of the architects asked Her whether She was "God", to which She replied: "We all are 'God' ... potentially".

"In 1968, shortly before the Inauguration, my Grandfather, Andre-da (Andre Morisset), announced to me that Mother wished that I, along with my cousin Kalya, should represent Auroville for the Inauguration. I jumped for joy of course, and waited for my mother, Janine, to arrive home to give her the news and ask her for her permission, because I was just 16 years old at the time and children were not allowed at all to miss school in France. In fact at the time I definitely couldn't have missed school, but for the fact that I was hoping to make a career in ballet and had started practicing 6 to 8 hours a day. For that purpose, a few months earlier I had registered as a student to the prescribed Correspondence Course which allows children to study at home with much more flexibility in their schedule. Thanks to that I was able to come to Auroville and participate in the ceremony.

"When I arrived I stayed at Pournaprema's place, at that time above Navajata's house by the Ganesh Temple. There was a lot of excitement, and much going to and fro to Mother and asking Her opinion for all sorts of details. Everyone was very busy, visiting the site at Auroville and discussing how the ceremony would unfold. But there was never any stress or confusion. Everything seemed to happen very smoothly, and I don't remember any chaos or stress, except for one incident where Vincenzo was in charge of building the Urn that would contain the samples of soil from all countries. It was not going well. He had to accept the fact that the only way to build it was to cut the marble slabs into very small pieces and then glue them back together onto the surface of the Urn ... what a job! He went on ceaselessly for days and struggled quite a bit, till it came at last to be the beautiful lotus bud that we see today.

"There was also a lot of activity setting up a large exhibition at what was called then the "Bureau d'Auroville", with beautiful photos of the land, information about Auroville, and models of the future town and various projects. That exhibition was set up in the part of the school building facing the Ashram that later become Pourna's house and was named "Aurore".

"The day before the inauguration Kalya and I went to Mother and received from Her the box, lined with silver paper, that contained the soil of Auroville to be poured last into the Urn, on top of the soil from all the other countries. I was carrying the beautiful flag of Auroville. There was a lot of wind, and a lot of strength was needed that day to hold the flag steady, but someone from the Physical Education Department had shown me exactly how to hold it – may he be remembered gratefully right here! – and everything went well.

"Of course you must know that when a country could not send a representative with soil, its soil was replaced with salt, and children of the Ashram school acted as representative for that country. All children and representatives went to Corner House for meals, and there was a very happy and lively atmosphere there too.

FRANCE

I wonder whether any of the representatives ever followed up and maybe came back to Auroville?

"I stayed on until the month of July, and then went back for more ballet training in France. Although I was supposed not to miss even a day of ballet training, I had stopped for months! I hadn't even thought of going back to France at the time, the atmosphere was so lovely, until my mother came to take me back. I then went into serious training for modern ballet. Later on I was privileged to teach ballet to many lovely students at the Ashram School.

"Being so young I didn't have any other responsibility but to carry the flag, so I cannot give you any more details. I can only say that I am so glad and grateful I was there, and would gladly live that experience all over again, and again, and again…

"Something really wonderful is there even now in Auroville, hopefully not only "in spite of us" but because of our love, aspiration and trust, and the growing awareness that, if nothing else, we are endowed with a deeper and more valid way of looking at Life, Ourselves and Others."

Varaghagiri Venkata Giri V.V.Giri, President of India and his wife, together with Roger Anger, Chief Architect of Auroville and Navajata, Chief Executive, S.A.S and Auroville, on the right B.D.Jatti, Lieutenant Governor of Pondicherry, sitting under the Banyan tree, 23 October 1969

It will be excellent

Extract from filmed interview of Kireet Joshi...

"Mother has said that she has 3 steps of action. The first, the establishment of the Centre of Education, the second Auroville, and the third Sri Aurobindo's Action. This statement of hers corresponded with my feeling that Auroville represents a major action of the Mother on Earth. On one occasion I had taken my students by bus to Auroville, and the whole way there we were shouting together, "We shall build Auroville!" It was as if all the time Mother was here in my heart and she had given me enthusiasm for Auroville.

"When Auroville was to be inaugurated in February 1968 I wrote a letter to the Mother, saying that we would like to offer some services towards the development of Auroville. She responded in French, "It will be excellent. Up to now I have not told you to work for Auroville because I thought you were very busy with school work, but it will be very nice if you take charge of all the youths that are coming for the inauguration." So from that day I took charge of all the youths that were to come, and accommodated all of them in Ashram houses.

"On one occasion I took the opportunity of taking them all out to Auroville at around 9.30am, near the time set for the inauguration. There was an unpleasant problem that arose, details of which I won't go into now, but that night at around 1.00am I heard the Mother say to me to go to Udar for solving the problem. In the morning I went to his house. He was ready to talk at 5.00am, and was able to sort everything out immediately, answering my questions.

"I must say that the children of the school helped tremendously in preparations for the day. At one time we had the idea that we would start the schooling in Auroville with some of our students from the Ashram, but then there were some difficulties, so that could not be done. Meanwhile I had been taking some of the applications to the Mother to join the Centre of Education, but she said that instead they should go to Auroville to start the school there. That was again an indication that she wanted to make a new experiment in education."

Also, in a text written on Roger Anger's death, Kireet wrote…

"I did not have many occasions to be directly in touch with Roger, but whenever I met him I always found in him a genius whom one could not fathom and yet a friend, in the waters of whose affection one could easily swim. My sphere of work was far removed from Auroville, and although I felt a tremendous admiration and intimacy with the developments of the work relating to Auroville, the only time I got the opportunity to get interwoven with a major programme of Auroville was when the Mother assigned to Tanmaya and me the task of organizing the participation of the youths who were to come to Auroville for depositing token soil from their respective countries in the foundational Urn on the occasion of the inauguration. The inaugural ceremony was to take place on the 28th February 1968. This task had intimate connection with Roger, because he was the living spirit behind the numerous activities that were connected with the gigantic inaugural ceremony.

"In my own personal life and in my sadhana, this occasion was momentous. All the arrangements of the youths had to be done in Pondicherry, and it was my responsibility to ensure that all the youths assembled at the right time at our Centre of Education so that they could be transported by buses which were to be furnished by the Sri Aurobindo Society. Roger was to receive the youths at Auroville, and the rest of their participation in the ceremony was under the charge of Roger. Thus Roger and I had to synchronize very carefully many aspects of this work. But how greatly I was shocked when the Sri Aurobindo Society informed me late in the evening of the 27th February that the buses, which the Society was to arrange for transportation of the youths, would not be made available to me, and that I should make arrangements on my own. This was a terrible disabling breach of their promise, and it put me in a grave state of crisis.

"This is not the occasion to narrate this incident in detail, but as can be imagined I would have failed miserably to transport the youth from Pondicherry to Auroville and to hand them over to the charge of Roger at the appointed hour. I almost failed. But I was seeking earnestly some miraculous help from the Mother. I knew no transport agency, and none whom I approached was better in this respect. Something seemed to be helping me to remain very quiet. It was about 1.00am that I could reach some deep level of being, where I heard the Mother telling me, "Go and meet Udar". I went immediately to his residence, but it was naturally all closed. It was too late to wake him up at that late hour, so I waited to 5.00am before knocking on the door of his residence. Fortunately Udar, whom the Mother had described as a "man with golden heart", understood my predicament and promised to help. The time available to him was so short that it seemed impossible he could do anything. And yet, miraculously, he succeeded. At 8.00am the buses arrived at the gate of the Centre of Education. The time left for me to arrange was extremely short. But I received maximum help from Tanmaya and teachers and students of our Centre of Education. I gave some anxious moments to Roger, since there was considerable delay in transporting the youths to Auroville. Nonetheless, Roger, although extremely anxious, showed no impatience when he received the youths along with me at the site of the inauguration, and outwardly nobody could detect any external sign of the delay that had occurred. Everything happened punctually, and when the Mother's inaugural message came to be relayed from Her room at Pondicherry, there was perfect calm and serenity, and nearly five thousand people who had gathered on that momentous moment of the inauguration got enveloped by a vibrant and gentle breeze of ineffable delight at the creative moment.

"It was Roger who had designed and created the beautiful Urn in which the youths were to deposit the token soil of their respective countries and were thus to gather the entire earth in that unifying vessel of the foundation of Auroville. It was Roger who had beautifully designed the pavilions around that vast ground of the inaugural site for all those who had assembled to witness that great moment of the birth of Auroville. The entire organization of the programme, the sequence and the punctuality of every unfolding moment, were meticulously executed, and it was evident that Roger manifested palpably and concretely the Divine Mother's power of perfection, particularly the genius and skill of Mahasaraswati. I cannot forget the smiling and shining face of Roger as it seemed to me floating over the entire movement and scene of the inauguration. Yes, "the Man of the Project" was spread from that Banyan tree (at the Centre of Auroville) to all the spreading circumference of Auroville."

One of the most interesting weeks in my life

Manju Jhunjhunwalla, who represented Rajasthan, remembers...

"On 27th February 1968 I received a note from Kireet Joshi informing me that I will be representing Rajasthan in the Auroville inaugural ceremony.

"I was thrilled to be part of the Mother's dream project.

"It was many years ago but it seems as if it was only yesterday.

"Early morning of 28th February 1968, dressed in my best skirt, I hurried to attend the ceremony.

"Delegates from all over the world had gathered there. The Africans stood out in the crowd with their vibrant coloured dresses and arrogant statures. With a gathering of delegates from different nations, it was like witnessing the entire world in a concise form on the Auroville soil. The ceremony was heralding a new era of world unity.

"The Mother read out the Charter of Auroville in French from Her room and it was broadcast live. Her words were directed to 5,000 or more people gathered around the Amphitheatre. Thereafter the Charter was read in 16 languages. "It was when Amritada read the Charter in Tamil that I understood how sweet the Tamil language was.

"When my turn came I walked slowly around the Amphitheatre and moved towards the Urn, carrying the soil in my hands. But just as I was putting the soil in the Urn I felt one of my sandals snapping. I walked barefooted back after placing the soil in the Urn, leaving the sandals where they lay.

"The banyan tree standing in an expanse of sun-baked earth was a quiet witness to this ceremony and all the happenings.

"Three delegates, one from Mauritius and the other two from Kenya, were lodged in my house.

"The week before the ceremony was a hectic one. There were a series of meetings held in the courtyard of the Ashram Library, which is a neighbouring building from my house. I participated there in the brainstorming sessions to explain to the delegates the raison d'etre of Auroville and its UNESCO link.

"One of the most interesting weeks in my life."

Auroville is anything but a miracle, a series of miracles

Prem Malik remembers...

"I had come from a management background. I was a manager in a multinational, and had come to Pondicherry for the Inauguration on 28th of February. On the 27th evening I was in Nava's house, where all the activities were centred, and believe you me I felt total bedlam. I was absolutely certain that there could be no Inauguration ceremony the next morning. So when I went back home (I was staying with some relatives here in Pondicherry), they asked me, and I said: "No, there can be no foundation ceremony tomorrow."

"But the first miracle that hit me was that next morning. We were supposed to leave for the site of the Auroville Amphitheatre, and at 6:00am the buses were there to take people there. And it was a terrible job to do because nearly 5,000 people had to be transported. They had come from all over the world, and to the Ashram, and they had to be transported to the site of the Inauguration. When I left the house and went up towards the Ashram, it was so silent. I said to myself that Mother had called off the whole thing. And then when I went further up I found there were queues of people, hundreds of them, very quiet and very calm, marching into the buses and being transported. I was absolutely amazed. My own experience of the world outside is that when you have so many people, people are trying to rush into the buses and there is a lot of noise. Yet here nothing, absolute peace and calm, and all of them were transported to the site without any difficulty. And I was stunned absolutely, because that was my first direct experience of a miracle. I had never seen one in my life

before. How she managed it is incredible. And then not only were all those people transported there, the seating arrangement there and the food, everything went off so beautifully. As if some power felt in the background was organizing everything.

"The only mishap that occurred was also my personal experience, in the sense that Mother had given me the job to look after the diplomats. There were about 25 of them from different countries, and I went on a caravan with them to the site. There all the seats that were reserved for these diplomats had already been occupied by the senior Ashramites, so they had no place to sit. So even miracles sometimes go haywire. But it was a beautiful experience. And after that there were a series of other miracles, so many of them, which I feel should be put on record in a book form, because I don't think that Auroville is anything but a miracle, a series of miracles."

The Mother took all the decisions
Dayanand Jamalabad remembers...

"The most difficult work was to lay the road to the Amphitheatre. Bits and pieces of land had been bought but they were not contiguous. So first of all the land had to be bought to connect the Kuilapalayam road to the land on which the Amphitheatre was going to be built. Truckloads of red earth had to be sent to the site, and work went on for a whole month. A system was devised to keep track of all the trucks which were taking the earth. I would send the truck driver with a chit, and when it reached the site the person present would write on it that he had received the material, and then the driver would come back to Pondy and take the payment for it in cash. This meant that I was called at all odd hours by the drivers who had come to take payment. In

those days all payments for everything were made in cash.

"The work of making the Amphitheatre and road was also given to the students of the Ashram School. I saw the Mother almost every day to keep her informed about everything or to get her latest instructions.

"My work during the ceremony was to help manage the crowds. Many villagers and the panchayat heads were invited. There was a huge crowd of people who had gathered that day, and as I spoke Tamil and I knew all of them I had to manage them.

"The villagers had never seen anyone else other than their own village people. They saw some foreigners when the Auroville project was started. When they saw me coming to them to buy the land on behalf of Auroville they saw me as someone working in collaboration with them. Although they had sold the land because they were financially gaining from it, they were suspicious about what it was going to be used for and therefore hostile to me.

"The Mother took all the decisions. She had asked me to plant 12 Transformation trees around the Amphitheatre. I did that, but later someone chopped them down.

"The banyan tree was in very poor condition. The villagers used to tie their cows to the tree, seeing it as just another 'village' tree. We started to look after it, and it began to look more beautiful from then on.

"The Mother was in a hurry, and was always saying: "This has to be done right now. There is no time." Something was descending, and she needed a place for it to manifest.

"The idea of having the Matrimandir just there was not planned until quite a bit later."

A boy and girl represented every country

Tapas Bhatt, who represented Syria, remembers...

Tapas, who comes from a (Baroda) Gujarati family, all of whom already had, and still have, strong connections with Sri Aurobindo and the Mother, was attending the Ashram School at the time of the inauguration.

For several weeks she remembers that the whole Ashram was focused on the coming inauguration. In the week leading up to the actual day the school was closed, and Tapas and others were coming up by bus every day to the Auroville plateau, alongside Roger Anger, as preparations for the event progressed to culmination. When it came to the big day she recalls the following.

"There was a strong police presence all the way from the SAS Office to the inauguration site, the roads all the way barricaded off to other traffic to facilitate safe and uninterrupted flow of the many VIPs and dignitaries (maybe some Ambassadors, cultural attachés, etc, plus of course the many Indian VIPs).

"All those chosen to represent a country were assembled at the SAS Office around 8.00am and then bussed out to the site (maybe 50 or so buses were involved in all to transport the 5,000 or more people) via Nehru Street, Jipmer, Certitude corner as it is today, and then a long, straight, newly made dirt road to the banyan tree via open fields with only a few palmyra palms off to the side of the road.

"The event started at 10.30am, and ended around midday, after which food was served near the banyan tree. First, Mother was heard reading the Auroville Charter, after which it was read in some 16 languages. Mother's "Dream" was also read out. Finally everyone was back at the SAS

Office in Pondy around 1.30pm, where Nava addressed us.

"The Urn was already in place where it is today, but the Amphitheatre was only shaped at that time by a raised earth circle demarcating what is today its perimeter, where sunshading had been erected to protect the crowd. People sat wherever they wanted, though one section had been reserved for the VIPs and another for the boys & girls representing each of the 124 nations, who one by one went forward carrying the flag of their country and its earth sample to place in the Urn. Each pair then went to join the others who had already placed their earth in the Urn, creating a colourful mass of national flags together at one strategic point.

"A boy and girl represented every country. Many were from the actual country, but others were Ashram students assigned to either join a boy or girl from the actual country or be the pair representing that country in the case of countries that had sent no-one. I represented Syria, my elder sister Chetana represented Panama. For those countries that had not provided a soil sample, salt was placed in the Urn instead, the salt of the ocean symbolizing the substance/element that links the shorelines of most of the countries around the world.

"The whole event and its preparation was wonderfully organized and conducted, mostly by way of the Ashram students and young people, who also directed people on site on the day. Overall the event was quiet, with no music background.

"My strongest impression was created by the gathering together of 5,000 or more people in that wide open landscape, in the middle of nowhere, where there was nothing but village fields, to start something of great significance for the future of humanity. I felt

without the slightest doubt that my whole future then lay with the Auroville project, that I had to start taking part in whatever way I could from that moment onwards."

(In course of the next few years following the inauguration some 30 young Ashramites like Tapas moved up from Pondy to take up life in Auroville.)

The Mother asked my father to involve himself in the construction of the Amphitheatre

Partha Hariharan on the role of her father...

"In 1963 my father (Hariharan) asked the Mother's permission to marry my mother (Hena), which she gave. That is how She came to know about my father. Then when the plans were made to construct Promesse, She asked Nata to ask my father to work for the project. My father joined Nata, and together they built Promesse (I think it was 1966/67). The Mother next asked my father to involve himself in construction of the Amphitheatre site, which had to be ready for the Inauguration in February 1968. He supervised the entire work, and completed it in 2 months with the then available tools and work force.

"Being Tamil, he also acted as interface between the villagers and Auroville in resolving disputes between them. The villagers at that time were unsure of the intentions of the work going on, and they had to be convinced about it. Many times they would come in groups and try to stop the work, and my father would have to deal with them and pacify them so the work could continue.

"Finally, on 28th February 1968, with Her Blessings, the Auditorium with its Urn was ready for the Inauguration."

We were creating the "New" World

**Interview with Maurice Shukla,
who represented Iceland...**

Q. How were you chosen to participate in the inaugural ceremony of the foundation of Auroville on 28th February 1968?

A. Serendipity, pure and simple, you might say. The delegates from Iceland could not make it in time, we were told, and so there we were, Vishakha and I. I was simply thrilled beyond words to have been given this amazing privilege, almost by default. In hindsight, I am always amused by the Mother's sense of humour and irony. I, who detest the cold, was chosen to represent Iceland! And that very year, just a few weeks later, on asking the Mother for a new name (I was exasperated by my friends mercilessly and endlessly distorting my original name) She called me Maurice! To me it rather suggested "More ice", making me an even worthier representative of Ice-land!

Q. Were you also involved in the preparations that led up to the event? If so, in what way?

A. Well, I was barely thirteen, so my involvement in the preparations was purely at a personal level. I spent a lot of very happy time with the delegates who had arrived – chatting, finding out about our mutual life-styles and routines and experiences, and eating with them at the Corner House. I still remember the fun and cheer sitting under the mango-tree at the Corner House in the evenings, chatting away endlessly and wanting the time never to end.

Frederick Buxloh visiting the exhibition under the Banyan tree

Q. Can you say something about the atmosphere in the Ashram in the month that led up to the final day?

A. It was simply, indescribably enthusing! As youngsters we had been fed at school and at the Ashram on the power and joy of "dreaming", and in those days for all practical purposes school and the Ashram felt like ONE WORLD. The excitement of launching this project of 'human unity', the colourful happy presence of all these international delegates from outside Pondicherry and outside India, the uncontrollable euphoria of creating the 'New World' which we felt was just around the corner, and around and above all this the tremendously reassuring and inspiring Presence of the Mother emanating from her room above the Samadhi: we seemed to be living in heaven already, and the gift of Auroville was that extra drop that spilled over onto an ocean of gladness!

Q. Can you share with us your memories of the day itself? What were your impressions?

A. Unbelievable excitement was in the air, lots of movement and joy linking us all, unstoppable chatter amongst us kids, smiles that just would not leave our faces, our School where we were supposed to gather and be picked up from had a truly 'international' dimension to it. Auroville that day seemed but a natural culmination of this amazing coming together of Sri Aurobindo and the Mother; the East and the West were meeting after all in this celebration of our being ONE FAMILY! As the buses drove us towards Auroville, the way seemed endless, full of all kinds of vehicles heading for this momentous Inauguration of the New City. I remember the bare red treeless terrain, the heat and the powdery Auroville dust in

the air that we could see from the bus, and the sea of visitors that had already gathered as we reached the Banyan Tree and the Urn area where the ceremony was to take place. Here all frontiers and barriers seemed to disappear as this sea of humanity mingled in all its diverse colours and shapes. I remember how even the Tamil villagers who had come from all around felt so much part of what was happening on their dusty plateau that day.

Q. Did you meet any VIPs? If so, how was your interaction with them?

A. VIPs? We all felt like little VIPs that day! Who was bothered about "VIPs" on the 28th? How could the Mother's Dream have hierarchy? We all felt to be an equal part of that special day's events.

Q. What were the highlights of the day, from your point of view?

A. First, obviously, there was the inaugural ceremony itself. The way it had been planned, organised, all very disciplined, systematic, the flags, the spiral pathway to the Urn, the neatly designated seating arrangements, the smartly dressed Ashram volunteers in white... And then as the ceremony began, hearing the Mother LIVE from her room in the Ashram! That was one incredibly powerful moment for me: She was with us, amongst us, through that live broadcast. We felt the ceremony was taking place in Her womb! Wasn't it the 'birth' of a new world?!

Then as kids we were so excited about reading the name of the country that was being announced, and to try and recognise the delegates. Suddenly I realised

A special free tea supply vehicle

**Realisation of the new creation
(Realisation of Auroville)**

It is for this that we must prepare.

**Power of success
(Success of Auroville)**

The power of those who know
how to continue their effort.

how many we were from the School. I remember Kalya and Fabienne very clearly, representing Auroville, looking so inspiringly young and beautiful, and both were, besides, directly connected to the Mother as well. And then to see our dear Nolini-da sealing the Urn at the end. No-one more fitting could have been chosen for this highly symbolic charged act. The unity of the world had been established in the heart of the earth itself, eternally rooted.

Q. Did you feel that something "special" was happening? If so, can you say something about it?

A. Absolutely! We were creating the "New" world; we were the sun-eyed children of a marvellous Dawn, the flaming pioneers, the barrier-breakers, the architects of this incredible world of oneness that we lived and breathed that day and in the days preceding it. I felt the Ashram was expanding its horizons; it was embracing the whole world. Another very strange feeling I had was this: though Auroville was officially coming into existence on 28th February 1968, I had the unmistakable impression that it had ALWAYS been there, waiting for us to come and discover it. Thank god, the 'sponsor-tag' of 'Sri Aurobindo Society' had completely disappeared in the background in that euphoria of new creation. It didn't feel like some individual's or an organisation's project but a project of the entire earth, something that the planet had been yearning for, for all these centuries. And the Day had at last dawned!

The atmosphere was vibrating

Poppo Pingel, who represented Germany, remembers...

In 1967 I was working in Osmania University Engineering College in Hyderabad, when at Christmas time I was given a biography of Sri Aurobindo in German, which I didn't immediately read.

I had also met Carlos, who was then Germany's Consul General in Madras (now Chennai). When he learned that I was an architect he said, "You know that they are building a new town, an international town, near Pondicherry," and he asked me if I would be ready to go there. I said "Yes".

Next, in January 1968, when I was overseeing the building of a school in Bihar, I got a telegram from the German Consular office in Delhi which read: "Go to Auroville for the Inauguration, if Principal agrees." He did, and so I booked my flight from Hyderabad to Madras.

In awareness that I would be coming in contact in Pondicherry with the Ashram of Sri Aurobindo, I decided to start reading the book I had been given on him, and was continuing to do so during the flight. Unexpectedly, I found it fascinating; I was even getting ripples and goose pimples on my skin as I read certain inspirational passages.

On arrival in Madras they put me in a hotel, from where I went to the Consulate to meet the German girl also invited for the inauguration from our organization, Petra Erdmann, who was a nurse in the Nilgiris. Together we then went to the old bus-stand in Chennai and took a bus to Pondy, loaded with a substantial sum of money for the 5 days we would be there; much more than I had been accustomed to getting for my work up north.

At the bus-stand I met the first person from the Ashram, Bibash Mutsuddi, a nephew of Nirodbaran. We talked all the way to Pondicherry. They dropped me at Corner House, from where a Mercedes car driven by Udar drove me to Shyama and Frederick's house in Pondy. I liked the old colonial atmosphere, the beer, coffee, baguettes, the colonial French roads, the beach – I loved it all. Vincenzo was there also, in and out, and Swapna. I felt very comfortable with everything, but the German girl I had come with told me that she felt ill at ease.

One morning we were called to practice how to put the soil into the Urn in an alphabetical line, A B C etc. All the 124 national representatives had to line up; which took time. I had been given the German soil in Madras, flown in by Lufthansa I think. In line I was close to the French, F coming just before G, so we started talking. There was a creeper with blue flowers near the Foyer du Soldat. I went there to pick some flowers, small bell-shaped flowers, and gave some to the French people while keeping some myself. I then placed my two flowers in the French soil and they put their two in the German soil. We had been always enemies for so long, and the mutual gesture felt symbolic; it was very strong.

Then came the actual Inauguration day. We boarded the bus, four or five buses with the hundreds of representatives. From Jipmer onwards there was nothing:

Poppo Pingel and Petra Erdmann representing Germany

a desert. Edayanchavadi was a sleepy village of mud huts. Otherwise there were just fields, with probably peanuts, and occasional palm trees in line defining their edges. You could see all the way from there to Pondicherry.

Next we stopped in the middle of nowhere and were told to get out. It was about 10 o'clock, already hot, though there were some shaded stands. We had to sit there. The atmosphere was vibrating. I could feel the enormity of it all. I was young, I had just been called to be invited to participate, but the greatness of that moment... What I did feel was the human unity, the international atmosphere, like what you may feel in the Olympic Games, but there it is very much vital while here it was bright, it was of another quality. People told me, "We need people like you with Indian experience."

After the inauguration, around 1 pm, we went back to Pondy feeling very thirsty. I went on to Quality Hotel, where we had a few drinks in addition to water, and I got a bit tipsy.

We were nicely taken care of by the Ashram during those five days. Lunch, dinner, all organized at Corner House. I liked the people there, the international atmosphere. But then it was back to Madras for the return flight to Hyderabad.

My heart throbbed in happy anticipation

Arup Mitra, who represented Thailand, remembers...

"The novel idea of collecting the earth from all the countries and pouring it into a single Urn to signify world unity was unique and innovative. The laudable idea came from the Mother, and no other ceremony could have

better symbolized the foundation of an international city. Then, there came a rider. When, during the first period of Wednesday the 28th of February 1968, we were asked to assemble in front of Room 7 in the school courtyard, one of my classmates excitedly whispered into my ear that a girl and a boy from among us would represent such countries as had only sent their earth, but not their delegates. In those days of reticence, the thought of sharing the dais with a girl was thrilling. And my heart throbbed in happy anticipation.

"Soon, I was joined by a shy, large-eyed smiling girl of my age named Aruna Nandi. We were designated to represent Thailand. Happily, that long morning gave us ample opportunity to come to know each other better. As a first step, we introduced ourselves as best we could during the exciting trip to the barren land which had just been named Auroville, in an overcrowded convoy of buses such as we had never seen before. Then, surrounded by an indescribable multitude of people, came a romantic wait under the cool shade of coconut keet sheeting before the beginning of the earth-pouring ceremony, during which we were able to drift a little closer to each other.

What finally bonded us together was the concluding lunch at the Society House, overflowing with noisy delegates from all over the globe. When nearly nine long years later Aruna Nandi became Aruna Mitra, the foundation structure of the Matrimandir was peeping out above ground level, the barrenness of the red land was giving way to lush forestation, and Auroville itself was becoming a destination for international seekers of peace and spirituality.

Inaugurationday of Auroville, M.P. Pandit, Basappa Danappa Jatti, Lieutenant Governor of Pondicherry, and Navajata, Chief Executive, Sri Aurobindo Society and Auroville

States of India:

Andaman & Nicobar, Andhra Pradesh, Assam, West Bengal, Bihar, Chandigarh, Delhi, Goa, Gujarat, Haryana, Himachal Pradesh, Jammu & Kashmir, Kerala, Laccadives, Madhya Pradesh, Madras, Maharashtra, Manipur, Mysore, Orissa, Pondicherry, Punjab, Rajasthan, Uttar Pradesh

Names of countries:

Afghanistan, Albania, Algeria, Argentina, Australia, Austria, Belgium, Bhutan, Bolivia, Brazil, Bulgaria, Burma, Burundi, Cambodia, Cameroon, Canada, Central African Republic, Ceylon, Chad, Chile, China (Communist), China (Nationalist), Colombia, Congo, Congo (Kinshasa), Costa Rica, Cuba, Cyprus, Czechoslovakia, Dahomey, Denmark, Dominican Republic, El Salvador, Ecuador, Ethiopia, Fiji*, Finland, France, Gabon, Germany, Ghana, Greece, Guatemala, Guinea, Haiti, Honduras, Hungary, Iceland, India, Indonesia, Iran, Iraq, Ireland, Israel, Italy, Ivory Coast, Jamaica, Japan, Jordan, Kenya, Korea, Kuwait, Laos, Lebanon, Liberia, Libya, Luxembourg, Malagasy, Malaysia, Mali, Malta, Mauritania, Mauritius, Mexico, Mongolia, Morocco, Mozambique*, Nepal, Netherlands, New Zealand, Nicaragua, Niger, Nigeria, Norway, Pakistan, Panama, Paraguay, Peru, Philippines, Poland, Portugal, Qatar, Quebec, Rhodesia, Rumania, Rwanda, Saudi Arabia, Senegal, Sikkim, Singapore, Somalia, South Africa, South Yemen, Spain, Sudan, Sweden, Switzerland, Syria, Tanzania, Thailand, Tibet*, Togo, Tunisia, Turkey, United Arab Republic, Uganda, United Kingdom, Upper Volta, Uruguay, USA, USSR, Venezuela, Vietnam, Yugoslavia, Zambia.

*listed in the Ashram papers as not-independent territories

Auroville and UNESCO

We in UNESCO have tried other ways of living together and we have seen them ending in stark tragedy ... We have tried in UNESCO, in the UNESCO world, which represents the pluses and minuses of humanity, which represents the world as it is, and not the world as it can be, or should be – we have tried every way, and we have failed.

And so now we turn to Auroville, and to its foundations, the firm foundation on which its human unity, its universal harmony, is to be built. That foundation is Man ... Man in all his glory, in his divinity, in his unfathomable depths which he can reach, and which Auroville will make it possible for man from everywhere – from Africa, from Europe, from Asia and from the Americas – to achieve. It

is not surprising therefore that UNESCO has embraced Auroville as a programme which embodies its major and fundamental purposes...

Education, which is the special domain of UNESCO, which deals with men's minds, with men's spirits – even education as it has so far been practiced – has not led to peace, has not led to harmony and understanding.

The people who start wars are not the illiterate or the ignorant in Europe or America; the people who burn buses and trams in our country are not the illiterates, and since the torch-bearer of this confusion is the educated elite, UNESCO's responsibility for seeing what kind of education should be developed is an urgent one. When I spoke of Auroville as being a hope, I had this very much in mind.

The Auroville system of education, by the way, is not a paper plan; it is already being worked out in the International Centre of Education of the Sri Aurobindo Ashram in Pondicherry. The educational system that Auroville will have, which is now already being developed and perfected, is the system in which every man, woman and child will learn to live, and live to learn, freely and harmoniously ... in a world which is frighteningly progressive.

It is the Aurovilians whom I met who are the basis of my hope. They remind me of the astronauts and the cosmonauts, who as you know, spend years training themselves for the tremendous task that they have to undertake. The Aurovilians are the cosmonauts and astronauts of this new international city of hope, of development, of prosperity and of charity. And it is their spirit which I have seen for myself, the training which they are undergoing, and the concrete pilot-work which they are doing now in actually digging the foundations of this great city, that are for me the basis of what you can call my hope for Auroville.

The first task is for every member-state, and every man, woman, and child in the member-state, to understand Auroville as the international city where the ideals that we have been so long seeking for, of peace and harmony, of human unity, will be realised – realised very concretely, not simply as resolutions, as declarations, flag-waving, but through the schools, through the colleges, through the workshops, through the factories, through the farms and through the international airport which will bring men and women from all over the world. So the first thing that UNESCO will help member-states to do, and is already

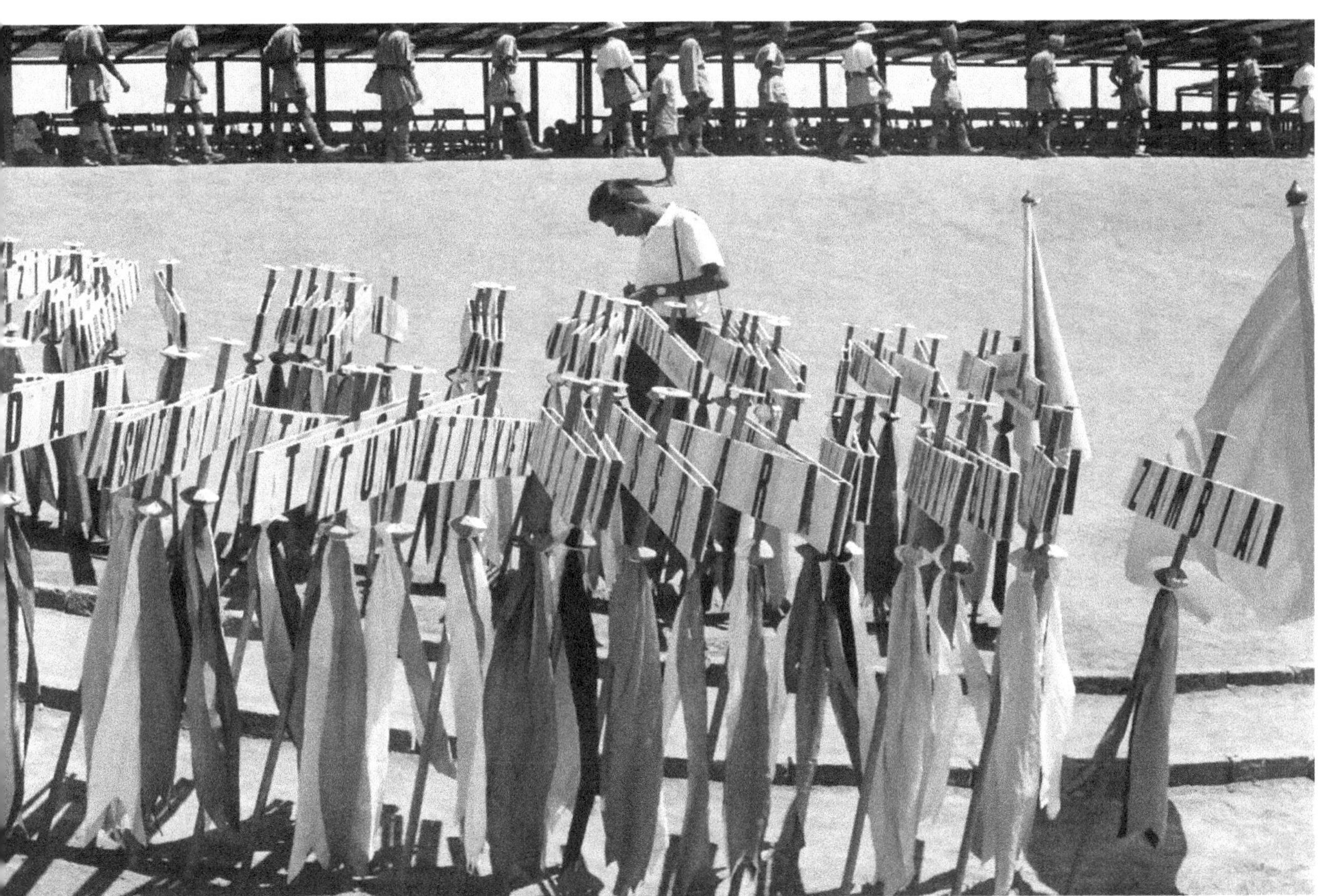

doing, is to understand the Auroville programme, and then see what of this programme would be the responsibility of a government, or an organisation, or a university, or an individual. We are proud of the fact that most of the member-states of UNESCO sent part of their soil, exactly a year ago, for the foundation ceremony. That symbolic action in giving a part of their land, land over which man through the ages has fought, fought bloodily, fought at the cost of lives, in the creation of a new city is a hopeful augury of the time when UNESCO and all its member-states would make their contribution – financial, material, and spiritual – for the building of Auroville.

Equals One

On behalf of UNESCO, on behalf of all of you
present here, and not present here,
I hail Auroville, its conception and realisation,
as a hope for all of us and particularly for our children,
for our youth who are disillusioned
with the world that we have built for them
and who will find in Auroville a living symbol,
inspiring them to live the life to which they are called.

Malcolm S. Adiseshiah,
Deputy Director General of UNESCO, on 28.12.1968

Follow up meeting with Dr. Malcolm S. Adiseshiah at the Sri Aurobindo Ashram Library, with Medhananda.

The Vision and the Soul

Earth needs a place where men can live away from all national rivalries, social conventions, self-contradictory moralities and contending religions; a place where human beings, freed from all slavery to the past, can devote themselves wholly to the discovery and practice of the Divine Consciousness that is seeking to manifest.

Auroville wants to be this place and offers itself to all who aspire to live the Truth of tomorrow.

20.9.1969

Auroville:
At last a place where one will be able to think only of the future.

January 1967

At last a place where one will be able to think only of progressing and transcending oneself.

At last a place where one will be able to live in peace, without conflicts and without rivalries of nations, religions ambitions.

At last a place where nothing will have the right to impose itself as the exclusive truth.

February 1968

Auroville
La ville dont
la terre a besoin.

The city the earth needs.

The purpose of Auroville is to realise human unity.

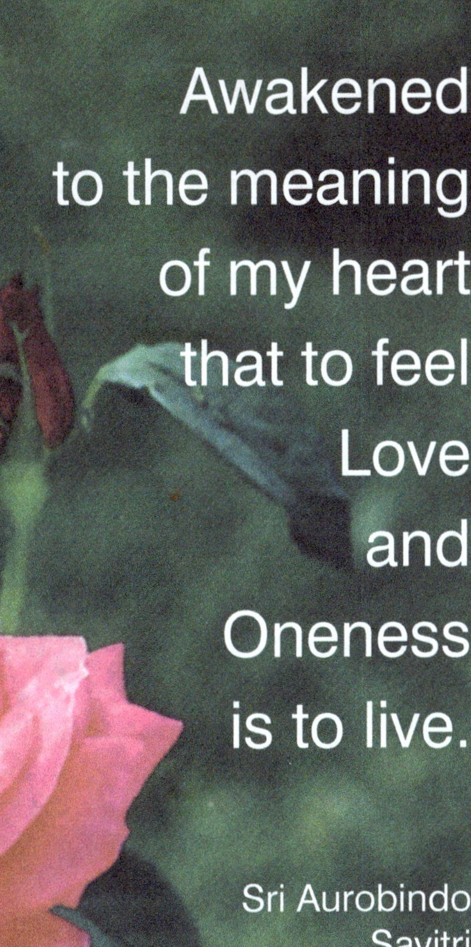

Awakened
to the meaning
of my heart
that to feel
Love
and
Oneness
is to live.

Sri Aurobindo
Savitri

Love for the Divine
The vegetal kingdom gathers its most beautiful
possibilities to offer them to the Divine.

Contact details

General information on Auroville:
info@auroville.org.in

Public/media relations:
outreachmedia@auroville.org.in

Auroville International website:
www.auroville-international.org

Auroville website:
www.auroville.org

Acknowledgements

Photographs:
We thank the Auroville Archives for making it possible to use photos of Auroville's early years.

We also thank the Sri Aurobindo Ashram Archives for use of their photos.

Paolo Tommasi: p.6-12,14,17,19,23,33-35, 77,99,101,107,109-111

Designed and produced by:
PRISMA, Aurelec-Prayogashala
Auroville 605101, Tamil Nadu, INDIA
prisma@auroville.org.in
Tel: +91-413-2622296
Fax: +91-413-2622185

Concept & Layout: Franz Fassbender
D.T.P. work: S. Janarthanan

© PRISMA
ISBN 978-81-928152-5-1
First edition: 2018

Printed at:
Sudarsan Graphics, Chennai, INDIA

Text:

pp.6-12	Sri Aurobindo, The Divine Life, B 2, Part 1, pp.1053-1055
pp.14-19	Equals One
pp.20-26	Words of the Mother-1, CWM 2nd Ed., Vol. 13, pp. 25 1-58
pp.33-35	February 7, 1968, Mother Agenda 1968, Vol 9 - pp. 50-53
pp.39-40	Mother's Agenda, February 3, 1968, pp.41-42
pp.49-53	The Auroville Experience
pp.61-62	Auroville-The City of New life, pp.143-146
pp.69-71	AV Today, February 2003, No. 169
p.74	Mother's Agenda , 28 February 1968, Vol.9, pp.67-68
pp.76-77	Mother's Agenda , 28 February 1968, Vol.9, pp.69-70
pp.80-83	AV Today, February 2003, No. 169
pp.85-89	AV Today, February 2003, No. 169
pp.91-96	AV Today, February 2003, No. 169
p.143	AV Today, February 2003, No. 169 Malcolm S. Adiseshiah, Deputy Director General of Unesco, Equals One, 1969-3, Auroville the Universe City
pp.144-146	Equals One, 1969-3

Other publications

Auroville Architecture
towards new forms for a new consciousness

Auroville Form Style and Design
towards new forms for a new consciousness

Landscapes and Gardens of Auroville
the transformation of the land

Front Cover:

Inauguration of Auroville, 28 February 1968

Back Cover:

Dawn bonfire at Auroville's Amphitheatre

Flap inside back Cover:

Matrimandir, Amphitheatre

Photos on right:

(clockwise from top left) Wooden bullock carts were the only vehicles of transport in those early days; Inauguration of Auroville; Matrimandir and Banyan Tree; Matrimandir, Banyan Tree, Garden; Entrance to the Matrimandir; Child goatherds near the future Amphitheatre and on the road to Aspiration

www.ingramcontent.com/pod-product-compliance
Lightning Source LLC
Chambersburg PA
CBHW060232120726
48009CB00004B/241